MASARYK
IN ENGLAND

I. THE NEW PRESIDENT (1919)

MASARYK IN ENGLAND

BY

R. W. SETON-WATSON

CAMBRIDGE: AT THE UNIVERSITY PRESS
NEW YORK: THE MACMILLAN COMPANY
1943

PRINTED IN THE UNITED STATES OF AMERICA

To

JAN MASARYK

I dedicate
these memories of his Father,
in the hope
that his fortitude in exile
may serve as an encouragement and example to
the rising generation of Czechoslovaks

PRAVDA VÍTĚZÍ

CONTENTS

page

Preface ix

CHAPTER I

Thomas Masaryk, the Man and the Statesman 1

CHAPTER II

Masaryk in England 33

Masaryk's Message, 33. My First Acquaintance with Masaryk, 35. Our Meeting at Rotterdam, 38. Memorandum on Conversations at Rotterdam, 40. Rough Notes, 48. Secret News from Roumania, 50. Ernest Denis, 51. Masaryk in Rome and Geneva, 55. Some of his Daily Jottings, 58. He Comes to London, 60. First Efforts at Propaganda, 61. 'Independent Bohemia', 63. The Hus Centenary, 64. London University, 68. Suspect to the Police, 74. Masaryk as Candid Critic, 75. The Need for a New Weekly, 86. 'The New Europe', 88. Rough Jottings ('Peace Terms': 'Signa Temporis': Lloyd George as Prime Minister: Wilson's Note to the Belligerents: A Life and Death Struggle: Wilson's Ideas), 89. Report of Vojta Beneš on Voska's Work in U.S.A., 96. Masaryk and the Russian Revolution, 101. Masaryk and Bolshevist Russia, 104. Masaryk and Wilson, 112. The President-Elect in London, 114.

CHAPTER III

Independent Bohemia 116

(Masaryk's Confidential Memorandum of April 1915)

CHAPTER IV

The Problem of Small Nations in the European Crisis 135

(Inaugural Lecture of October 1915)

CHAPTER V page
At the Eleventh Hour 153
(Masaryk's Confidential Memorandum of January 1916)

Index

ILLUSTRATIONS

1. The New President (1919) *facing title page*

2. Milan Štefaník (1918) *facing page* 22

3. Edward Beneš (1921) 56

4. Masaryk at Lány (1934) 114

PREFACE

The preparation of this volume was undertaken in the summer of 1938, at the request of friends in Prague. It was to have appeared in Czech only, in the idea that anything relating to the great President's career would be of interest to his compatriots, and that many details of his two years' activity in England still remained unknown: an American edition was also planned. The downfall of Czechoslovak independence, following upon the shameful Pact of Munich, rendered publication impossible. But to-day the situation has changed beyond recognition. A Czechoslovak Government, under President Beneš himself, has been set up in England and officially recognised as the ally of the British Government, the remnants of their army are training in our midst, and Czech airmen are adding their quota to the splendid achievements of the R.A.F. The Czechs are no longer 'a people of whom we know nothing', and in many quarters there is the keenest sympathy and interest in their cause. Hence it is but fitting that attention should be drawn to the intimate connection of Masaryk, the founder of their modern liberties, with our own country at the height of the Great War—a connection prepared by long study and natural affinities no less than by the political exigencies of the moment.

Though I shall always regard it as one of the great privileges of my life to have enjoyed the friendship of two such men as Thomas Masaryk and Edward Beneš, I should have preferred to keep my own name out of the narrative, as not in any way relevant. But I soon found that this was not possible, that my correspondence with Masaryk, and the Memoranda which I Englished and distributed for him, contain certain essential clues to his work in England in those decisive years, and deserve to be placed on record once for all.

These memoranda (see pp. 63, 83 and 153), which were intended for a very restricted circulation and not at all for the general public, contain certain obvious faults of style, which were almost inevitable under the circumstances. I did not feel entitled to make even verbal changes after a lapse of 25 years, and they are therefore printed as their author passed them for the printer. Nor has any attempt been made to curtail, omit or explain away certain passages on the military situation of 1915 which reveal their author as the citizen of a landlocked state.

One of Masaryk's spiritual forerunners, John Amos Comenius, turned to England at a critical moment in his career. The two years which the exiled Masaryk spent in England laid the foundations upon which he was afterwards to build up American recognition and the symbolic declaration of independence at Philadelphia. And in a not too distant future, I fondly hope and believe that the second President of Czechoslovakia, Edward Beneš, will set forth from England to the task of Czechoslovak liberation and reconstruction.

R.W.S.-W.

1 *December* 1942

CHAPTER I

Thomas Masaryk, the Man and the Statesman

The career of Thomas Masaryk is without any parallel in modern Europe. That the son of a coachman on an Imperial Habsburg estate should in his old age have played a decisive part in the disintegration of a great Empire and should then have restored his country to independence and unexampled prosperity and presided over its destinies for seventeen crowded years—this is in itself sufficiently remarkable, but does not in itself differentiate him from those other men who from humble beginnings have achieved leadership. Masaryk was essentially a leader who planned further ahead than his contemporaries, but who also understood the corroding effects of power, the vital need of restraint in the ruler, and above all the need for taking the nation into his confidence, educating it in the sense of drawing out all its innate qualities and sharing its manifold aspirations. In every sphere of life he built upon a basis of belief in God's justice and confidence in the principle of 'consent of the governed'.

The following essay is in no sense a biography, but mainly an attempt to throw into high relief the salient features of his career. Born on 7 March 1850 at Hodonín (Göding) in Moravia, he was educated at Brno (Brünn), Vienna and Leipzig, and after three years as 'Privatdozent' at Vienna, was appointed in 1882 to the Chair of Philosophy at the newly created Czech University of Prague, and filled it for thirty-two years. He was also a deputy in the Austrian Parliament from 1891 to 1893 as member of the Young Czech Party, and from 1907 to 1914 as leader of the small group of Czech Realists. He was also editor of the literary review *Naše Doba* and later of his own daily newspaper *Čas*, and was the author of a number of philosophical and historical studies. After the outbreak of war, he took four months to think out and mature his plans, and in December 1914 he went to Italy and finally broke with the Habsburg Monarchy, becoming early in 1915 Chairman of the Czech National Council. While the Council's headquarters were established in Paris under Beneš, he himself remained in London till May 1917. He arrived in Russia after the first Revolution, in time to organise the Czech Legions, and then, after the Bolsheviks seized power, crossed Siberia to America and exercised a decisive influence upon the plans of President Wilson in the last summer of the Great War. That autumn at Philadelphia he launched a Declaration of Independence, drafted on the American model, and in December he returned from America to Europe as President-elect of a free Czechoslovak Republic, recognised as such by the Allied and Associate Powers. For seventeen years he presided over its destinies, from the old castle of the Habsburgs above the city of Prague.

His life, thus briefly summarised, falls into three great divisions, first as teacher of the nation from 1880 to 1914, second as leader of the national cause from 1914 to 1918, and third as 'Pater Patriae' from 1918 to 1935. He was already sixty-four when he assumed leadership of the nation, and eighty-five when the first serious signs of failing health prompted him to resign the Presidency. Only his Spartan manner of life could have enabled him to resist the strain so long.

It is obvious that such a career is incomprehensible without some knowledge of the milieu out of which he came: and without launching upon any elaborate historical survey it is necessary to point out certain essential tendencies in Czech history which are not merely of yesterday. In the first place it may be freely admitted that the country of which Masaryk, more than any other man, was the founder or *Restitutor*, reflected in its very name two rival tendencies. For it was a reconstitution of the old historic Kingdom of Bohemia, on the basis of historic right, and yet it united with it, on the basis of the principle of nationality, Slovakia, which had been an integral part of Hungary, save for passing interludes, ever since the invading Magyars overthrew the so-called Great Moravian State in the ninth century. It may quite reasonably be argued that there is a certain contradiction in this. Its makers were from the outset fully conscious of the fact, and knew that the problems which faced them were more than usually complex, but also that their successful solution might perhaps set a genuine and lasting European precedent for states of mixed nationality.

Secondly, Bohemia's whole history and evolution have been determined by the fact that it occupies the very centre of the Continent, as a Slav salient into German territory. But it is necessary to add the emphatic reminder that this was due, in the first instance, to a long process of successful Germanisation in the territory lying to the east of the Elbe and the Oder. Till then Bohemia was not a salient at all.

As a result of this aggressive colonising policy of Germany, to which she is consciously reverting after six hundred years, Bohemia has always, of all the Slav nations, been the most exposed to Western and especially to German influences. From the fourteenth century onwards its history has centred around the conflict between Czech and German, though both races have learnt much from each other and have, despite their quarrels, had a much longer record of fertile co-operation than is sometimes assumed. There has been much intermingling of blood: and it is interesting to note in passing that one of the latest commentators on the tragedy of Munich, Mr Maurice Hindus, who is of Russian-Jewish origin and has a personal knowledge of Russia, is continually stressing in his book, *We shall live again*, the contrast between the two Slav nations, Czech and Russian, and what he regards as certain un-Slav traits in the former. But though it may well be that German infiltration has left its traces and perhaps added the same sort of stiffening to the original Slav stock as the Nordic element has imparted to the Celtic populations of Northern Britain, we are none the less entitled to regard the Czechs as perhaps the most valuable intermediary between East and West: their role in the Russian question during and since the Great War might be quoted as an illustration.

If we look at the physical map of our Continent, we see Bohemia as a rough-shaped diamond at the centre—a diamond which has written certain indelible lessons on the windowpane of Europe. Bismarck once spoke of Bohemia as 'a natural fortress erected in the centre of our Continent'—a phrase often quoted in recent months. But it is well to continue the quotation. 'Bohemia', he said, 'in the hands of Russia would be our enslavement. Bohemia in our hands would be war without mercy or truce with the Empire of the Tsars.' Here is one of those sayings which show what a big man Bismarck really was—despite all his brutal *Realpolitik*, capable on occasions of great restraint and balance. His fanatical successors have held up the first half of the phrase to Europe as a justification for their policy of conquest and absorption—wilfully ignoring the fact that Czechoslovakia's alliance with Russia was purely defensive and was planned as an Eastern Pact to which Germany was free to adhere. For a time Hitler's dupes shook their heads over 'Czech aggression' as exemplified in an essentially defensive alliance. But the full extent of his duplicity became apparent in August 1939, when he himself, fresh from the destruction of the most Russophil of all the Slav nations and already poised to attack another Slav nation which had preferred his alliance to that of Stalin, did not scruple to combine with this very Stalin, on whose regime he had for years poured forth torrents of abuse and frenzy. It was a crime for the Czechs to seek insurance in Moscow, but for him it was a perfectly legitimate stroke of high policy to ally himself with what he called 'this scum of humanity'. And the bewildered Nazi sheep accepted this *volte-face* as a matter of course, and continued to denounce the 'hypocrisy' of Britain and America.

Bohemia, it should be remembered, is one of the earliest examples of the national state in Europe. She also has a great cultural tradition: for Prague was the first University of all Central Europe, founded in 1348, and was for a generation the equal of Bologna, Paris and Oxford—not merely German, as is falsely alleged, but divided into 'Nations' after the fashion of the great mediaeval international schools. She also had a great religious tradition in the Hussite movement, which established principles commonly known as Protestant, a whole century before the Reformation. She led the van in the struggle for liberty of thought at the Council of Constance and, in the words of Bishop Creighton (whose account of the movement is in many ways still unsurpassed), 'it is the glory of Hus that he first deliberately asserted the rights of the individual conscience against ecclesiastical authority'. The influence of Wycliffe's teaching upon Hus is well known and forms the first serious historical contact between England and Bohemia.

Hus, however, blended the religious reformer and the national leader to a peculiar degree, which explains his influence to-day in what is mainly a Catholic country, proud of those other traditions associated with St Wenceslas, Duke of Bohemia and with the famous Slav apostles Cyril and Methodius.

It is typical of the crass misconceptions put about by German propagandists, that they should talk of Hussite Bolshevism and try to link up two essentially different concepts. In so far as this is not deliberate, there exists an apt enough parallel in the attitude of the greatest of German reformers towards the Bohemian heresy of the day. But Luther, when he suddenly realised his error, declared with a frankness and rush of feeling all his own, 'We have all been Hussites unawares'. It should be added that Masaryk, in writing on the Czech Reformation, stressed its moral and humanitarian character, leading logically to political and social revolution. But he meant this not in a subversive sense, but as an original attempt to solve the problem of authority. Hence 'brotherhood' was the ideal and watchword of the most characteristic of all the Czech sects, the 'Unitas Fratrum' or Church of the Brethren, and its pacifist and democratic leanings, on lines not altogether dissimilar from those of the Society of Friends, were very marked.

To-day it is more than ever necessary to stress the cataclysmic character of Bohemian history. Is it mere accident or is there some deep underlying explanation of the undoubted fact that all the Slav states—Russia, Poland, Bohemia, Serbia, Bulgaria, Croatia, Bosnia—have these vast inequalities to show, culminating at times in national extinction? In any case Bohemia, after holding all Europe at bay in the early fifteenth century, and securing for herself an intermediate position between Catholic and Protestant, which lasted two centuries, fell at a single blow in the battle of the White Mountain in 1620. Speaking in the broad terms suited to so general a survey as the present, it may be said that Bohemia disappeared from the map for wellnigh two centuries, as effectually as Bulgaria and Serbia under Turkish rule, and more effectually than Poland under Russian rule. Under the triple tendencies of Centralisation, Catholicisation and Germanisation, pursued by the House of Habsburg, Bohemia became little more than a historical memory. Her constitutional liberties were suppressed, her nobility almost rooted out and replaced by strangers, her population decimated, her middle class reduced by the Thirty Years' War and by enforced emigration, her language banned from polite society and from the whole framework of the state, her literature systematically exterminated by the Jesuits.

Under such circumstances the Czech revival, faintly discernible after 1790, and gathering volume in the twenties of last century, was little short of a miracle. There is a famous anecdote that tells of the small group of patriots who met in a Prague inn, and how one said to the others: 'If the ceiling should fall on us, it would be the end of the Czech national movement.' This story has been denied: but it is symbolical of the truth. As the nobility, save for a few splendid exceptions, were alien or out of sympathy, and the towns to a large extent Germanised, the new movement had its roots in the 'petite bourgeoisie' and in the peasantry. From the first it was plebeian, essentially democratic, and its leaders were obscure scholars and thinkers, who counted for but little in their lifetime, but laid their foundations very deep. It is not an accident that the Czech movement has for centuries found its heroes among such men as these. Bohemia has, it is true, produced two statesmen of European rank—Charles IV (whom Hitler recently presented as a German monarch, but whose title to the throne of Bohemia came from his grandmother, the last scion of the ancient national Czech dynasty, and who was himself Slav in speech and impregnated with French culture) and again George of Podiebrad, whose project for a League of States has sometimes been claimed as the first purely political anticipation of the Genevan League. She also produced one soldier of genius —the blind general Žižka. But her true heroes have been Hus, the priest, the 'poor person' of Chaucer, the Rector of the University, and court preacher: Chelčický, the humble sectary preaching non-resistance—a true forerunner of Leo Tolstoy: Comenius, the pioneer of modern educational methods: then in the nineteenth century a group of seemingly obscure scholars, and in the twentieth, quite logically, Masaryk, Beneš and Štefaník, the triumvirate of savants who achieved Independence and Unity. Masaryk himself, speaking at the Quincentenary of Hus in Geneva, during the war, deliberately contrasted Chelčický and his idea of humanity and brotherhood with Žižka as 'representative of modern militarism'.

The revival came in three stages—first, from 1790 to 1848, came the revivers of the language, Dobrovský, Jungman, bearing the instruments for its use—the new dictionaries, grammars and philological studies which were its dry bones. Then came the men who knew how to use them—Kollár the poet, Šafarík the literary historian and archaeologist, the twin founders of sentimental and scientific Panslavism in its modern garb. Then Havlíček, the first Czech journalist and pamphleteer, and Palacký, the historian of Hussitism, who reconstructed his country's past in defiance of the censor and the Jesuits, and gave it back its heroes and its national pride.

The second stage was from 1848 to 1879—a period of brief constitutionalism, when Palacký attended an Austrian Parliament, but declined the invitation to the German Federal Parliament in Frankfurt and preferred to preside over a Panslav Congress in

Prague: then ten years of absolute repression followed by a period of political experiment, in which the Crown ended by throwing over the Czechs in favour of the Magyars, and creating the fatal Dual System, the cul-de-sac in which the House of Habsburg was to meet its death. In this period it was Palacký—from so many aspects Masaryk's true forerunner—who led the Czech nation, championed the State Rights of the Bohemian Crown and inaugurated the mistaken policy of abstention; who followed no revolutionary policy of separatism or revolt, but simply claimed a due place for Bohemia inside the Austrian Empire. It was Palacký who coined the famous phrase: 'If there were no Austria it would be necessary to create her.' That was the creed of the mid-nineteenth century, before the nationalities had lost all hope of Austria putting her house in order. But it was he too who struck a more radical note in that other phrase: 'Before Austria was, we were, and when Austria no longer is, we still shall be.'

The second stage ended in 1879, some years after Palacký's death, when Francis Joseph quarrelled with the dominant German Liberals, and, in his search for a new parliamentary majority, created the so-called 'Iron Ring' of Clericals and Slavs, and made certain national and linguistic concessions to the Czechs in return for their consenting to enter the Reichsrat.

The third stage, from 1879 to 1914, was the period of co-operation of the Czechs in the life of the Austrian state—a period in which conflict was always more in evidence than co-operation, and an astounding amount of mis-directed energy was expended upon the old German-Czech feud. The eighties and nineties were a period of furious racial strife, which had not merely a political, but a social, educational and economic side. It is only possible to allude here to two of its most essential features. On the one hand there was the progressive radicalisation of Czech political life—the Old Czechs of the sixties being driven back by the Young Czechs (the new bourgeois party) and they in turn by the Czech Agrarians, Czech Radicals and Czech Socialists. But despite much divergence of tactics and outlook, all showed an united front on any national issue in Parliament or outside it. And in sharp contrast to this there was the progressive disintegration of the German parties. The German Liberals lost their monopoly and were in hopeless rivalry with the Pan-Germans (who acclaimed the Hohenzollern and 'Los von Rom'), with the Clericals (afterwards Christian Socialists), with the Social Democrats, with the Radicals (who admitted Jews to their ranks, whereas the Clericals and National-Socialists rejected them). And as they never could all agree on vital issues, Parliament became a beargarden of catcalls and inkpots, and government by party came to be superseded by government by bureaucratic ministries and the notorious Paragraph XIV, which suited the dynasty only too well. And a further result was the progressive breakdown of the Dual System with Hungary.

Meanwhile outside Parliament the Czech movement steadily deepened in these thirty-five years. (1) The industrialisation of Austria affected both Czechs and Germans and brought new classes to the front. (2) The struggle for posts was waged fiercely, and the Czechs, year by year, increased their share. (3) An even fiercer struggle was waged in the educational field by such rival organisations as the Matice Česká and the Deutscher Schulverein. The Czechs appreciated, none better, the value of education, and by the turn of the century had all the secondary and primary and technical schools they required, had reduced illiteracy almost to zero and were virtually on a par with the Germans. Not least of all, they had their own University in Prague, side by side with the German, and rapidly made of it, of the Bohemian Museum and of the wonderful National Theatre (built and rebuilt out of the free subscriptions of the peasant and urban masses) so many centres of national culture and discipline. This essentially musical nation produced two great composers, Smetana and Dvořák, and a national opera based on 'folk music'.

Last, but not least, the Sokol Gymnastic societies founded in the sixties by Miroslav Tyrš, on an essentially democratic basis, spread what he called the 'philosophy of discipline'. 'By the education of body and spirit, by physical energy, by art and science, by all moral means, to revive the fatherland'—so ran the founder's programme: and those who know the role of the Sokols in these twenty years of freedom or who have ever attended one of their unforgettable congresses, know how well and truly the foundations were laid by the two previous generations.

To sum up: the Czech national movement had by the turn of the century followed out the lines already indicated. It was essentially a movement of the lower middle and peasant class: its weakness lay in the fact that it had to find and create its leaders as it went along, and that these leaders, lacking in the tradition of experience and political training, had to work out their own methods and learn through grave blunders. Its strength lay, then as now, in the fact that it was built from the bottom upwards and combined in fairly equal proportions the urban and agrarian elements.

This brief introduction was necessary in order to give some picture of the milieu, of the society, into which Masaryk was born. He was twenty-nine when the third stage indicated above was reached, and when the Czechs gave up political abstention and entered the Reichsrat. In 1882, when the new Czech University was founded in Prague, he was transferred to it from the junior post he already held in Vienna: and for over thirty years he was Professor of Philosophy there. The fact that Masaryk in this period acquired such a deep influence over the rising intellectual class (despite, or just because of, his strenuous, Spartan outlook on life) is, it may safely be affirmed, no mere accident. It reveals the strongly *ethical* basis of the new movement, despite obvious faults and exaggerations—a tendency which goes back to the Hussites and their dual religious and national tradition.

But it is important to note that his influence extended far beyond his Czech and Slovak compatriots and that as more and more Slavs from other countries came to the new and flourishing Czech University, they too, and especially the Croats and Serbs, fell under his spell, with very notable political results.

In philosophy his interest lay with the Western thinkers, especially with Locke, Hume, Comte, Stuart Mill: but social and religious problems were always of the first importance with him. In one of his talks with Karel Čapek he says: 'I overcame the Slav anarchy in myself by the help of the British philosophers Locke, Hume and other empiricists.' His inaugural lecture at Prague was on 'Hume and Scepticism'.

The other half of him, however, clung to Slav models. Brought up as a devout Catholic, his mind moved towards Protestant individualism. But meanwhile he was always at once fascinated and repelled by Russian mysticism and philosophy, and began a prolonged study of the Russian mind, of which the fruit is to be found in his epoch-making book *The Spirit of Russia*. His early outlook is revealed in one passage, where he insists that the Redeemer of Mankind was 'neither a politician, an economist, a Socialist nor a demagogue. The way in which, amid the political and social unrest of his time, Christ keeps aloof from politics, is truly sublime.' The book performs the function of a pioneer: it is a revelation equally of Panslavism and Slavophil ideas, of 'the Third Rome' and what he calls Caesaropapism, of Bakunin and other prophets of revolutionary anarchism, of Marxism in its Russian form, of the dissolvent effects of German Protestant theology and philosophy upon Russian Orthodoxy. He claimed to have found in the study of Russia and Russian literature the true significance not only of Feuerbach and Hegel, but even of Hume and Kant. This study was bound up with the problems of decadence and degeneracy which already overshadowed Europe as he wrote on the eve of the Great War. It was sober and realist to the last degree: as Masaryk once said to Čapek, 'I have no more use for empty talk about Slavism than I have for flag-wagging patriots'.*

* In the first period of the war I found myself in possession of the only copy available in this country of *Russland und Europa*: whereas I was credibly informed that more than one German war bureau of the first importance kept this book on its desk for constant reference. The excellent English version of Mr and Mrs Paul only appeared in 1919.

Masaryk's keen social interest had long before this led him to lay his finger on one of the sores of modern life, and his essay on *Suicide as a Social Mass-Phenomenon* (in 1891) was the result. This was the first of his writings to arouse acute controversy: for a long time afterwards it was misrepresented—or, I should prefer to think, genuinely misunderstood—by the extreme Clericals as irreligious and atheistical, though this was the very reverse of the truth. The fierceness of controversy between Clerical and anti-Clerical in the eighties is shown by the fact that the Cardinal of Prague denounced Masaryk to the Emperor Francis Joseph as a seducer of youth and advocate of suicide. In actual fact he stressed Religion as the best antidote to suicide (in passing, it is interesting to note that he regards the low rate of suicide in Scotland, in spite of counter-tendencies towards drunkenness, as due to an innate religious sense). At the very moment when prominent Catholic clergy accused him of blasphemy and atheism, he was writing these words: 'The religious question is really the only one I know of.' As an old man, at the height of his career, he was to write: 'Jesus, not Caesar, is the meaning of history.'

And here it is surely permissible to interpolate a few plain words to the address of Nazi propagandists and their dupes in this country, who write and talk of 'Hussite Bolshevism' and speak of Masaryk's disciple and successor Beneš as a subversive and anti-Christian element, working for the Bolshevisation of Europe. This is said advisedly, for it would be possible to name persons of influence and position who have put this view across certain of our politicians, who ought to know better. Two points will suffice for refutation. Beneš, working in fullest accord with Masaryk, was responsible for the 'Modus Vivendi' with the Holy See, one of the most enlightened modern contracts between Church and State. Since then the relations of the Vatican and the Czech Foreign Office have been consistently cordial, and the present Pope's estimate of Beneš as a statesman, if it could be published, would greatly surprise the calumniators of the ex-President. And it is based on the personal knowledge acquired by the then Cardinal Pacelli in direct diplomatic dealings with the Republican Government in Prague. Moreover, those who know anything of the Millenary celebrations of St Wenceslas in 1929, of the Eucharistic Congress in Prague in 1936, or who saw the kneeling crowds at President Masaryk's funeral, know how grotesque the charge of Bolshevism is. On the latter occasion the radio address, delivered by President Beneš before the Diplomatic Corps and the whole world, again deliberately reverted to and adopted the saying of Masaryk, 'Jesus, not Caesar'.

Masaryk's critical faculty was employed just as strongly in the opposite direction, and his book on *The Foundations of Marxist Theory*, written many years before Marx became the infallible prophet of the Russian Revolution, deserves more attention than it has received. In one of his talks with Čapek he summed up very succinctly his whole attitude. 'Marxism', he says, 'is an economic theory and philosophy, particularly a philosophy of history. Economic theory, like every other science, is a matter for scientific investigation, revision and improvement, and Marxian theory, like any ther, must be open to criticism and free consideration....Revolution or dictatorship can sometimes abolish bad things, but they can never create good and lasting ones. Impatience is fatal in politics.' He flatly challenged Feuerbach's view that 'the heart makes a revolution, the head a reformation', on the ground that only a bad psychologist separates heart and head. But, he goes on, 'to Marx, as to the whole Hegelian Left, Reformation is not sympathetic—not merely the Christian one, but the whole principle'. Masaryk is ready to wait and holds that reform takes generations, and that revolution can best be averted by work.

Meanwhile, from the first, Masaryk's study of the great thinkers was extended into literature, and led him to test the philosophic outlook of Goethe, Nietzsche, Victor Hugo, Zola, and perhaps above all, Dostoyevsky, in whom he recognised the key to all that is most ideal and most unbalanced, noblest and most destructive in Russian psychology. His third Russian volume, on

Dostoyevsky, which is still in manuscript, was planned under the title 'A Struggle for God—Dostoyevsky and Nihilism'.

Events slowly but surely drove the philosopher and thinker into public life, and forced him to apply to the affairs of the world that Realism which he was evolving as his philosophy of life. We have his own testimony, confirmed by all who knew him well, that he kicked against the pricks, that he did not enter the limelight gladly. Providence, we may confidently affirm, was guiding him along a path which he had not chosen. But when he told Čapek that he was not a fighter by nature, that genial, true-hearted humanist, who had not the heart to survive the liberty of his country, surely must have smiled incredulously. Those of us who worked with him may be excused for thinking that here the philosopher was not reading his own mind with his usual clearness and detachment. Many a time in the war I myself have seen the fighting spirit in him defy the most desperate situations. I remember him one day, as he left my house, quoting the blunt phrase of Rieger, the Czech leader of a previous generation. 'We won't give in.' No more, no less. No fine phrase here, but bedrock resistance. And this is true of every Czech to-day, since the Munich betrayal.

There are three especially famous illustrations of this evolution of Masaryk which are so revealing, so characteristic, that no estimate of his career can pass them over in silence.

The first was his attitude to the so-called Koeniginhof and Gruenberg MSS (Královė Dvur and Zelená Hora are the less familiar Czech names). Discovered by Hanka a century ago, they were supposed to contain the earliest known poems in the Czech language, and were praised as epoch-making in the history of popular poetry in general. With the philologist Gebauer, Masaryk was above all instrumental in proving these MSS to be an ingenious but none the less impudent forgery. He was fiercely attacked by all the super-patriots for his unpatriotic deed. But he held boldly to the view that 'the truth shall make you free', and that forgery is a radically unsound basis for a national revival.

His arguments have long since been accepted as unanswerable. It is unnecessary to stress the cleansing effects of such candour upon public opinion and national sentiment, or to contrast the attitude of Dr Goebbels, who openly treats success, not truth, as the only serious criterion in national controversy.

The second example was Masaryk's attitude towards one of the most notorious Ritual Trials of the closing nineteenth century. In 1889 an unfortunate Jewish butcher's apprentice, Leopold Hilsner, was charged with the murder of a Christian child, and the hoary myth of ritual sacrifice was revived. It caused intense feeling, was widely believed, and led to anti-Semitic outbursts, especially in the class of the so-called 'kleine Mann' in Austria, the milieu of which Adolf Hitler is the most famous product. Masaryk protested in a brochure against the myth, boldly criticised the conduct of the trial and demanded revision. The public attitude to this disgusting story, he declared, 'wounded him to the heart'—'so much lack of judgement, lack of ideas, passionate over-haste and inhumanity to the pitch of cruelty' seemed to him an ominous sign of abnormality. He was hooted down and insulted at the University and had to discontinue his lectures for a time. But in the end his enemies were reduced to silence, and long before the war he had earned the gratitude of the whole Jewish world for his defence of justice against intolerance and crass superstition.

The third illustration, more purely political, was his attitude to the notorious Zagreb Treason Trial in 1908, which, according to pre-war standards, was one of the grossest judicial scandals of the age. It is but fair to add that, judged by the barbarous standards to which Europe has latterly been degraded, the whole affair was relatively mild! Everything is relative in this unhappy world of ours!

Masaryk lodged his protest in a resounding speech before the Austrian Parliament on the whole Croatian question, mercilessly exposing the Ban of Croatia and his subordinate officials, but also his prompters, the Government of Budapest. It is not uninteresting to note that when he reprinted the speech in pamphlet form, he prefaced it with quotations from Edmund Burke and Charles James Fox which are self-revealing, and show his contacts with English political thought. To-day they are more apposite than ever, and deserve to be quoted.

1. From Edmund Burke—'Refined policy ever has been the parent of confusion and ever will be so. Plain good intention, which is as easily discovered at the first view, as fraud is surely detected at the last, is, let me say, of no mean force in the government of mankind. Genuine simplicity of heart is a healing and cementing principle.' How true of Masaryk himself, twenty-five years later.

2. From Charles James Fox—'The experience of all ages and countries teaches us that calumny and misrepresentation are frequently the most unequivocal testimonies of the zeal, and possibly the effect, with which he against whom they are directed has served the public.'

3. He added a third quotation from a great Habsburg—the Archduke Charles. 'The Minister of a great State who degrades policy to the level of intrigue, is like a Prince who descends from the throne in order to beg in antechambers. We have seen both in our day, and shall do so again; because it is easier to play the part of a valet than that of a master.'

The motive force of the speech was moral indignation at such sordid and stupid illegality. But it put forward some highly practical theses: (1) Austria-Hungary, as the largest Southern Slav state, must give its Balkan policy another turn, in order to win over the Southern Slavs. This, he of course realised, meant solving Hungary's internal crisis. (2) Austria-Hungary must rely on the strength of her own peoples and must no longer follow an aristocratic racial policy, but must democratise herself at home and abroad.

One of the worst malefactors of the trial, the examining Judge Košutić, in the official organ of the Croatian Government wrote of Masaryk as 'a man without honour, a nobody, the refuse of human society', taking care to add that he used these eloquent expressions without having deigned to read the offending speech. Perhaps I can best bring home to you in one phrase the full scandal of that affair by mentioning that I was in Zagreb at the time, and found it ringing with details of how the presiding Judge and the Public Prosecutor, Tarabocchia and Accurti, night by night got drunk together in one of the principal cafés of the town.

Quite undeterred by insult, Masaryk continued his campaign and played a notable part in the Friedjung Trial, the sequel to this Zagreb scandal, in December 1909. Here in Vienna itself, the foremost Austrian historian of the day, on the basis of documents supplied by the Austro-Hungarian Foreign Office, set out to prove that a number of the most eminent leaders of the Serbo-Croat Coalition in Croatia were traitors in the pay of the Serbian Government. It was Masaryk who by his courageous persistence (and he did not hesitate to visit Belgrade in search of evidence) was able to prove that the documents on which Friedjung relied were forgeries, supplied wholesale to the Austro-Hungarian Legation by an out-at-elbows student named Vasić, and some of them actually doctored up in the Legation itself. The crowning sensation came at a session of the Austrian Delegation, when Masaryk challenged Aehrenthal to his face. Then, while the Foreign Minister remained stubbornly silent, Masaryk denounced Count Forgács, the Minister in Belgrade, as Count 'Azev'—a deliberate offensive comparison with the notorious Russian police spy who betrayed the police to the revolutionaries and the revolutionaries to the police.

Some of the most eminent of the Serbo-Croat leaders at this time were disciples of Masaryk, and in his Reichsrat speech he declared: 'For Supilo, Pribičević and Lukinić I would lay both my hands in the fire.' I remember very vividly his evidence at the trial. I as yet only knew him very slightly, and was still a little sceptical as to his political role: and as I listened in court, I felt as I was often to feel in successive crises of the Great War. There was in the man an austerity, a hatred of effect or of phrases, a deliberate rejection of all the arts of window-dressing, that repelled the unregenerate or the unconvinced. The spell he cast was the result of closer acquaintance: it came from sheer force of character, from an insistence upon realities and fundamentals, stripped of all verbiage or ornament. There was the same uncompromising note in his private life. No alcohol, no tobacco, plain living and high thinking: and here it is important to mention a vital influence and inspiration throughout his career in the gifted American lady who became his wife in 1878, who shared his ideals and his intellectual standards and handed them on to the next generation, and who lived to see him as Father of his Country.

These three examples may serve to show how irresistibly he was being driven into political life. The programme and tactics of existing parties did not satisfy him, especially the chauvinistic tub-thumping against the Germans and the over-emphasis so often laid upon ancient historical rights. In the early nineties he had had his first taste of Parliament and had not liked it. But in 1893 he founded a political review, *Naše Doba*, and later on *Čas*—first weekly, and, in the five years before the war, daily. In 1902 and 1907 he lectured in Chicago and Boston on an endowment fund provided by the late Mr Charles Crane, the Maecenas of many Slavonic and other Nationalist causes. In 1900 he formed a progressive party of his own, the so-called *Realists*.* They never secured more than three seats in Parliament, but his following among the cream of the Czech intelligentsia was infinitely more important than mere numbers would suggest: he enjoyed the sympathy of most of the Slovak Protestants and progressives: and his was by now a name to conjure with, a real moral force, in the wider Slav world beyond the Habsburg border—in Serbia, Bulgaria and Ukraine, even in Russia and Poland. To have no illusions on the real state of things—such was the motto of the new party and such was Masaryk's method throughout his life. Incidentally, he once said, 'I am a realist, but I like romance. I see no contradiction in this', and so Pushkin, Byron and de Musset were among his favourites. But he devoured Hardy,

* In conversation with Emil Ludwig he accepted the name of Realist—'das heisst, res contra historiam'—*Gespräche mit Masaryk*, p. 160.

Meredith, Galsworthy, Swinnerton, Lawrence and Katherine Mansfield. Masaryk possessed that quality which Goethe once called 'Exakte Phantasie'. His style was rugged and sometimes oppressive: but the presentment of his case commanded attention and was always inspired by vision and intellect. The confession of spiritual faith which he made to a puzzled and astonished Reichsrat in 1908, in connection with the case of Professor Wahrmund (the militant anti-clerical German-Austrian professor) marked him more than ever as a unique figure in the politics of the Dual Monarchy.

The gulf that separated him from the directors of Habsburg policy is best illustrated by an incident of 1913, when Masaryk, relying on the prestige which his role in the Zagreb and Friedjung affairs had given him in Serbia, re-visited Belgrade, discussed the whole situation with the Premier, Nicholas Pašić, and carried back a concrete offer of *rapprochement* to Count Berchtold, Aehrenthal's successor as Austro-Hungarian Foreign Minister. It is on record that Berchtold treated Masaryk with lordly contempt and thought he was out to make a little money!

In this connection it is perhaps worth pointing out that Masaryk (in this point agreeing with the other Czech leaders, but differing radically from the Slovak and Roumanian leaders in Hungary) had no belief in the Archduke Francis Ferdinand, and made no attempt to establish relations with him. All his information, from many confidential sources, led him to believe that the Archduke's relations with the Bohemian feudal nobility (to which his wife, Countess Sophy Chotek, belonged) would not work out advantageously for the Czech people, and again that the Archduke's state of health was already dangerously bordering upon madness. This must be stressed because one of the counts against the Habsburgs in Hitler's *Mein Kampf* is the alleged Czechophil outlook of Francis Ferdinand. It is only necessary to read the passages concerned to see that Hitler genuinely believes what he writes, but they provide one of the classic instances of his ignorance and unreliability in matters relating to his Austrian homeland.

Masaryk's point of view on the eve of war may be summed up very briefly. He distrusted the Habsburgs and all their ways: but he did not despair of an evolution in a federal direction—what was often called 'a monarchical Switzerland , in which all the many nationalities of Austria-Hungary would attain equal rights. But that seemed to him only possible on a democratic basis. He knew Tsarist Russia far too intimately to be capable of the astonishing *naïveté* of wishing for a Russian Grand Duke and Russian bayonets in Prague. Being a realist, and well informed, he knew the growing danger of war, especially in the Balkans as a result of Austro-Hungarian policy towards Serbia.

We have reached the turning point of August 1914. In so dreadful a situation Masaryk once more applied realist methods. He weighed his own decision many times, the price that his nation might have to pay, the sacrifices which might be required of him and his family. It was essential, in evolving a policy, for him to know two things—what were the real inner aims and prospects of the Entente, and how long the war would last. The tactics and prospects of Bohemia must vary enormously, according as the struggle was decided in the first winter in one way or another, or was fought out to the bitter end. Refraining absolutely from all expression of opinion, and taking advantage of his parliamentary immunity, he twice visited Germany and Holland and the second time established contact with the Entente. Here I can speak from personal knowledge, for I went over to Rotterdam to a secret meeting, spent two days discussing all possible details with him, and took back a memorandum for the Foreign Office,* and a lot of secret information, some of a sensational kind. The memorandum is really worth study: for it contains not merely his programme, but (save for certain minor points) an

* Otherwise it went only to Wickham Steed, who gave it to Delcassé; to Ronald Burrows; and to Paul Vinogradov, who gave it to Sazonov. I published it *in extenso* in No. 9 of the *Slavonic Review* in 1925. It will be found on p. 40.

uncannily accurate forecast of the New Europe that was to follow the war. It should be added that the knowledge that Lord Kitchener believed in at least three years of war had a decisive effect upon his plans. For he could then gauge the probable strain upon the framework of the Habsburg Monarchy and he knew that there was time for the educative campaign which would be necessary to convince the Allies of the true state of Austria-Hungary and the aims of the Czechs, Poles and Roumanians. He went home without the Austrian police being any the wiser as to our meeting.

In December 1914 he visited Italy and was preparing to return yet again, when a friend inside the Vienna War Office warned him that if he recrossed the frontier he would be arrested and perhaps executed. The die was cast. For exactly four years he remained in exile—first at Geneva, then from March 1915 till May 1917 making London his headquarters. During the summer of 1915 he was joined by a young lecturer in economics at Prague, Dr Edward Beneš, and the various very small groups of Czech exiles organised themselves. The Quincentenary of the burning of Hus gave him his first opportunity for a public demonstration. Then we persuaded him to accept a lectureship at King's College, London, and inaugurate the newly founded School of Slavonic Studies. Mr Asquith was to be chairman: his place was taken at the last moment by Lord Robert Cecil. This incident deserves emphasis, not only because of our local interest and pride in it, but because the theme of the lecture, 'The Problem of Small Nations in the European Crisis', was a programme and a prophecy. Its main theme was the existence of a danger zone, still fluid in a racial sense in the vast triangle between Germany, Russia and Turkey: the dangers involved in Pan-Germanism and the need for 'the organisation, not conquest, of Europe'—'no Herrenvolk, but national equality and parity'—the right of small nations, no less than great, to an independent existence and development, and the absolute compatibility of national feeling with internationalism. A month later there appeared the Manifesto of the

Czechoslovak National Council abroad—proclaiming Unity and Independence as its double aim.

Henceforth the propaganda lay in the hands of the triumvirate —Masaryk in London, Beneš in Paris and Štefaník, the young Slovak astronomer and airman who by his connections with the inner ring of French politics did so much to smooth his colleagues' path. Later on Osuský, a young Slovak advocate from Chicago, became their delegate to Geneva and Bern, maintaining contacts in all directions and especially with Prague. Their task was twofold: (1) To study the Allied countries and win their public opinion for the Czechoslovak cause. (2) To maintain contact with Prague in order to know the pulsebeats of the nation at home and avoid the danger of repudiation. This latter task was especially difficult after the wholesale desertions from the Czech regiments began on the Russian and Serbian fronts, and when the influence of the Austrian High Command led to numerous arrests and measures of general repression in Bohemia. The story of the so-called Maffia—the inner ring of Prague politicians who maintained contact with their friends outside by many strange devices —is one of the most romantic stories of the war. The situation became more acute when Dr Kramář, the young Czech leader and Russophil, Rašín, the future Finance Minister of free Czechoslovakia, Dr Scheiner, the Sokol Chief, Dr Alice Masaryk and Madame Beneš and many others were arrested.

All this time Masaryk made London his headquarters, first because he regarded it as the *political* centre of the Allies, just as Paris was the military centre, and secondly, because he very soon realised that British public opinion and even leading statesmen were entirely uninformed on all questions relating to Austria-Hungary and her peoples. His friends put him in contact with the Foreign Office and gradually with many representative men, to say nothing of the 'Intelligence' (to which, both in Europe and in the United States, the Czech organisations rendered invaluable services throughout the war). But Masaryk had his own methods of getting information. He made it his business

II. MILAN ŠTEFANÍK (1918)

to see all and sundry, he studied the gutter press, he read patriotic novels and pamphlets, he was always reading our representative novelists as the key to British psychology: he paid special attention to food prices and to the cinemas, to see what went down with popular audiences and how the portraits of politicians and others were received. In short, no detail was too trivial.

His main calculation in the first two years of the war lay as it were between the two extreme poles. He knew that if the Allies won at all (as he believed they would, despite Germany's marvellous organisation) the final issues would rest with the Western Powers rather than with Russia, and he therefore never approved Kramář's policy of waiting with folded hands in Prague for the coming of the Cossack liberator. On the other hand, he reckoned upon a Russia modernised by war, restoring Poland (though perhaps only as a vassal state) and having a common frontier with the Slovaks in Ukrainian or Ruthene territory: and he counted definitely upon this great Slav neighbour as the wall against which the young state could lean its back in the first difficult years. My memorandum of October 1914 contains the phrase: 'Such a new State will have two new neighbours—*autonomous Poland and Russia herself; and for the success of the scheme it is essential that Russia should directly border upon Bohemia.*'* He assumed that the present 'Carpathian Ruthenia' would be in Russia. This is the one point at which his calculations were wrong: he foresaw the first Russian Revolution long before other people: he could not foresee the second with all its dire results. But this only makes his achievement all the more remarkable, for his master-stroke, as we shall see in a moment, was the direct result of the first Russian Revolution and his skilful change of tactics.

This is not the place for an account of his manifold war activities: the facts are on record in his own remarkable book *The Making of a State* and in Dr Beneš's still fuller *War Memoirs*. The secret of the success of Masaryk and Beneš is found in their tactical realism. They made their diagnosis of the European

* See p. 45.

situation, worked to a programme (in a sense that can be said of no other statesman in the war), and were always at the right spot where decisions were being taken. The crowning instance of this was the decision of Masaryk, after the Russian Revolution brought into power his own Liberal friends like Milyukov, to go to Russia in May 1917. The result was the formation of the Czecho-slovak Legions out of volunteers among the many prisoners from the Austro-Hungarian armies on the Russian front. Others have told the absorbing story of how these Legions grew, why they wore as their emblem the Hussite Chalice and sometimes sang the Hussite battle hymn, how they were responsible for Brusilov's last victory at Zborov in July 1917, how they came into conflict with the Bolshevists after the second Revolution, resisted the attempt to disarm them, and eventually withdrew by rail into Siberia and so to Vladivostok. 'The March of the 70,000', as Mr Baerlein's book calls it, stands in history with Xenophon and Garibaldi for romance and achievement of the impossible. Its contribution towards delaying the dissolution of the Russian front and the complete transference of the German forces from the East, was duly appreciated by the Allied Staffs and created the atmosphere which slowly convinced Paris and London that the Czechoslovaks were in earnest and capable of forming and maintaining their own national State.

The second tactical achievement was the work of Beneš (in Masaryk's absence but with his approval) in promoting the Italo-Jugoslav *rapprochement* after Caporetto and the holding of the Congress of Oppressed Nationalities on the Roman Capitol in April 1918. It was the moral effect of this Congress upon the nationalities inside Austria-Hungary that did more than anything else to precipitate its final dissolution.

The third tactical achievement was again Masaryk's. Crossing Siberia with the advance guard of his legionaries, he passed via Vladivostok and Tokyo to America, was welcomed at Chicago by the Czechs and Slovaks of the United States, and reached Washington in time to exercise a decisive influence upon President

Wilson and his advisers, during the paper war of the summer of 1918 between Washington and Vienna on the subject of peace terms. The result was the deliberate modification of the famous Fourteen Points by the American Government, and the inclusion among its war aims of Czechoslovak and Jugoslav Unity and Independence. This, combined with the not quite parallel recognition accorded by the British and French Governments to the Czechoslovak National Council as a Provisional Government with its own army, was the herald of Austria-Hungary's sudden collapse, and the spontaneous formation of National Councils, central and local, among all her constituent national units. On 28 October there was a bloodless revolution in Prague thanks largely to the perfection of the Maffia's organisation; the Czechoslovak Republic was proclaimed, and on 14 November Masaryk was elected President, Beneš Foreign Minister and Štefaník Minister of War in the first Coalition Cabinet under Kramář.

On 20 November Masaryk left the New World, and nine days later was received in London with royal honours. On 21 December he returned to Prague, once more the capital city of a free Bohemia, and hoisted the presidential flag over the castle of the Habsburgs.

And so we come to the last and crowning phase of Masaryk's life. At the age of sixty-eight this exiled Professor of Philosophy —still, it is true, fresher in mind and in body than many a man of forty—is installed in the old castle of the Přemysl and Luxemburg Kings and the Habsburg Emperors, perched high above the magic city of Prague, with its mediaeval bridge and towers and its rococo palaces and churches. And, most astonishing of all, at this age seventeen more years of active constructive work are to be vouchsafed to him. A few of his compatriots would no doubt have preferred to see Karel Kramář, the inveterate pre-war Russophile, as their first President. But in reality there was never for one moment any serious candidate except Masaryk.

The Russian philosopher Losky, in a very profound study of

Masaryk's ethical and religious teaching, examines the question how such a choice was possible, and naturally enough stresses his attitude in the three affairs of the forged MSS, the Ritual Murder and the Croat Treason Trial. Then he goes on: 'But such a struggle against the dishonourable conduct of statesmen, against deeply rooted social prejudices or against distortions of the truth by national egotism and partisanship, can only be conducted by a man for whom the moral ideas and principles of a wider humanity fill the foreground of practical action. It was to such a man, a fiery patriot, yet free from national egotism, and putting humanity above party or nation or state, that the reborn Czecho-slovak State entrusted the Presidential powers. To appreciate this choice at its true value we must remember that it is possible to be a fiery patriot and a self-denying statesman and yet at the same time to trample moral principles under foot....' Masaryk, he adds, 'incorporates in himself an attitude diametrically opposed to the national egoism of such a politician'. For myself, I remember in the darkest days quoting as the proper motto for Masaryk, those lines of Russell Lowell:

> They are slaves who dare not be
> In the right with two or three.

But now the wheel had come full circle: he had the whole nation behind him, and was called to a task of reconstruction and consolidation such as has rarely fallen to the lot of any man. A nation which had lost its independence for 300 years was now ripe for freedom, but required constant guidance through the maze of thorny problems created by the difficult geographical position of the new State and the infinite dislocation caused by the war. It was Mr Nowell Smith who first spoke of Masaryk as a modern fulfilment of the Greek ideal of the 'Philosopher-King'.*

Mr Smith would undoubtedly disclaim any originality, and Masaryk himself, though he never had any false modesty, would

* In his admirable Liverpool lecture on 'The Teacher as Statesman'.

certainly have shrunk from such a compliment. Yet reflection will show it to be literally true, and it may be affirmed that a nation which selects such men as its leaders and heroes (and Masaryk was not the first example) not merely does honour to itself, but qualifies for a high place among the ranks of civilised nations.

Amid all the absorbing duties of office he found time to write a book—to which in its English setting Mr Steed has given the title of *The Making of a State*—one of the most remarkable of its kind in any language. For here is the philosopher, turned statesman, revealing the innermost workings of the whole national movement under his direction, and concluding it with a veritable confession of the faith upon which he hoped the New Europe would rest. Already in his pre-war book, *The Czech Question*, he had declared: 'Political independence is in itself no more than the means to a right national life: we have lost it as soon as we cease to live morally as a nation.' And now he declared that in assuming office 'It was clear to me that no state or policy can prosper, unless the groundwork be moral'. He declared his belief in democracy as the foundation of the new dispensation. 'Spiritual absolutism, the varied forms of Caesaropapism and of temporal absolutism by which religion has been misused, will give place to a more exalted morality, a higher degree of humanity and a loftier religion which will freely guide the whole of our public life. The ideal is Jesus, not Caesar' (p. 404). In his answer to an address of both Chambers on his eightieth birthday he reaffirmed his democratic aims in home and foreign policy and said: 'If there exist conflicts between theory and practice...democracy is for me discussion, and therefore compromise. I was always against political absolutism and its infallibility, and still nurse the hope that...we shall overcome the absolutist habits in which we were brought up. Democracy is the loyal recognition of civil personalities and the ensurance of their co-operation. And it is never and nowhere superfluous to bear it in mind that democracy must not turn to demagogy or be confused with anarchy. Democracy is the rule of the people, but there can be no government without obedience and discipline' (7 March 1930).

To this may be added his historical profession of faith: 'To me the Czech question is the question of human destiny, a question of conscience. I believe with Kollár that the history of nations is not the result of chance, but that in it is revealed a definite plan of Providence and that it is the task of historians and philosophers, the task of every nation to grasp this plan in the world, to recognise and define its own place in it, and in accordance with this recognition to engage in every kind of labour, even political, with the fullest and clearest knowledge possible. I do not of course think that it will be vouchsafed even to the most penetrating reason to discover of itself the plans of Providence, but I believe that in the sphere of culture to-day it is the duty of every thinker to act according to the precept of Kollár.' In another mood Masaryk asks the question: 'Can a man only be true to himself in a big nation? Are fearless men not born in small nations also? Are Machiavellism and lackeyism an indispensable weapon of the oppressed and weak?' He answers with an emphatic 'No. Even the small man can attain his aim without intrigues. He who knows how to work needs no intrigues. Life is a specially hard struggle for the small and weak, but its whole sense lies in the fact that only the weak always stood for justice.'

His constructive achievement in these critical years borders on the marvellous: but of course not even he could have done what he did without the help of many able collaborators. Above all there was Dr Beneš, who held the post of Foreign Minister uninterruptedly from 1918 to 1935, when he succeeded to the Presidency. As there is here a tendency to differentiate between Beneš and Masaryk, to the disadvantage of the former, it is necessary to insist upon the absolute harmony of views, alike in the theory and the practice of foreign policy, between the two men. Beneš had often to bear the brunt of a difficult crisis and to concentrate on his own shoulders the odium which must not be allowed to fall on the President, even though the President was the last man in the country to shrink from it. But it is not too much to assert that the continuity of tenure and of policy which gave Beneš for twenty years such a unique position in Europe, was due in the first instance to Masaryk's resolute support against every intrigue. In foreign policy the two men must stand or fall together: and in that term is included all the eminent services which were performed by Beneš at Geneva in the field of international negotiation and agreement, and which are too well known to need recapitulation here. But it must at once be added that there were many others—Rašín, whose currency measures were the forerunner of a financial stability unknown to neighbouring states: Švehla, the astute and able Agrarian leader: Šrobár, Hodža, Dérer and other eminent Slovaks: Krofta, the historian turned diplomatist, many practical workers in the economic and social sphere, a solid phalanx of teachers at the four Universities, a certain number of really able diplomatists abroad, and a growing number of social workers, among them the President's own daughter, Dr Alice Masaryk. In each of these spheres the influence of Masaryk could be detected—moderating, inspiring, correcting, insisting, wherever necessary, upon enquiry or reform.

In so brief a biographical sketch as the present it is only possible to indicate in a few phrases some of the directions in which his influence made itself felt. Throughout the formative period of 1919–20 he took a most active share in the drafting and shaping of the new Constitution, under which the President's own position was eventually fixed about midway between the American and the French model. The fact that he remained in continuous office for seventeen years, but had the wisdom to resign at the very moment when he at last felt his powers to be failing, may be said to have given a certain directive to constitutional practice, and created something in the nature of precedents. But of course the evolution was still incomplete when disaster supervened and converted the third President, a man of no political experience though of sterling character, into the helpless lackey of a brutal conqueror. One thing can already be said with some certainty, that the practice of twenty years had concentrated the main decisions of foreign policy into the hands of the President—the intimate collaboration, on a footing of equality, between Masaryk and Beneš being replaced by that between Beneš and Krofta, also intimate and cordial, but without any doubt as to which possessed the ultimate power of decision.

The weakness of the political system by which Czechoslovakia was governed for twenty years lay in the complicated party system, and no one was more conscious of it than the President. But the glib criticism sometimes put forward abroad overlooked the fact that the parties merely reflected the complex social and economic structure of the State. The difficulty could of course have been surmounted by the method of 'Gleichschaltung' or annulment of all parties save one: and that is what was actually done: two parties were allowed to survive Munich, and since the German conquest there is only one, and this entirely unrepresentative of feeling or opinion. But any such solution is diametrically opposed to Masaryk's whole philosophy of democracy, whose moral basis is 'brotherhood' and love of neighbour—ideas reaching far back through Hus and Chelčický, and the Brethren, into the innermost consciousness of the Czech people. To him democracy means 'the era of discussion', and without free criticism there can be neither knowledge nor democracy. But he was only too well aware of the many defects of parliamentarism and saw their remedy only in the political and moral education of the electors. While, then, in most neighbouring countries the franchise was ruthlessly faked and distorted, in Czechoslovakia, under his guidance, exact proportional representation of both sexes and of all races, with every possible safeguard of minority voters and effective checks upon corruption, was from the first made a reality.

An oppressive foreign tyranny makes it impossible for the moment to place fully on record the many-sided contribution of Masaryk towards making Czechoslovakia a model democracy in the heart of Europe, consciously willed and planned by the great majority of its people, or to show how full advantage was taken of the administrative and educational machine bequeathed by the much-abused Austria; how liberty of the individual, the press, association and assembly, were made a reality: how religious liberty, after the effervescence of the first two years, was greatly extended: how economic and financial readjustment was rapidly carried out, and on this solid foundation, land reform and an advanced scheme of social insurance were built up: how, not least of all, an admirably equipped and disciplined army was formed, on democratic lines which we should do well to imitate. There were other features of the new regime specially dear to Masaryk's own heart—the transformation wrought in Slovakia after the neglect of centuries under Hungarian rule, the difficult experiment of bringing neglected Ruthenia back to cultural values, to national consciousness and to the beginnings of material welfare. No one with personal knowledge of those two little countries will challenge the contention that a cultural achievement which had not its equal in Europe was wrought in these twenty years, and that its overthrow by three successive stages—the 'Diktat' of Munich, the so-called Award of Vienna, and the final freebooter's raid upon Prague—represents a long step backwards towards barbarism and decay.

It is on the human note that this sketch must close. Masaryk was a great thinker, so open to the call of public affairs as to leave much of his maturer thought half-drafted or unwritten; a great patriot to whom patriotism was never enough in itself, and to whom the brotherhood of man was a legacy from his own national past; a constructive statesman who used his opportunity to the full when it came to him late in life. But he was also the most human of rulers, who radiated dignity and benevolence, and whose intimate knowledge of popular psychology made him at least as much at home with the peasant woman in the market-place as with the student, the intellectual, or the foreign visitor. The pictures of him riding at the head of his army, or again accepting a bouquet of wild flowers from a small Slovak girl at some village fete, deserve to live in history. And as a last memory, there is the farewell funeral procession from the palace of the Habsburgs, through the streets of Prague to the village churchyard at Lańy, amid the silent kneeling of weeping crowds, bidding unconscious farewell to the ending of a Golden Age. We may recall his tragic words to Karel Čapek—'Perhaps in fifty years our times will appear to people living then in such a blaze of splendour that they will almost envy us.'

Alas, his words were prophetic. The prison bars have closed upon our Czech and Slovak friends. We cannot speak to them: we dare not write to them. They are temporarily condemned to helpless passivity in face of plunder and intimidation: and there are many thousands in this country who felt a sense of poignant grief and shame at its share in the downfall of Czechoslovakia. But we know that the name and example of Masaryk are indelible memories which no persecution or misfortune can erase: and we can only re-echo the words of Comenius, uttered in the darkest days of Bohemia's downfall three centuries ago, and quoted by Masaryk at the beginning of his inaugural message to the liberated nation in 1918:

> I too believe before God, that after the storms of hatred brought on our head by our sins, have passed, the conduct of thine own affairs shall return to thee, O Czech people: and in this hope I make thee heir to all I ever inherited from my forebears and preserved through these grave times, but also whatever good things I may have added by the work of my sons and the blessing of God. All this I bequeath to thee.

The pathetic farewell phrase of Charles Dickens—'Lord, keep my memory green'—need never be applied to Thomas Masaryk. So long as the Czech nation exists, and is able to endure persecution and injustice, Masaryk will live in the hearts of every man and woman to whom the Czechoslovak Republic was a symbol of liberty and progress. His calm and steadfast religious faith, his austere philosophy of life, have made of him in the truest sense 'the Father of his Country', a shining light to all generations.

CHAPTER II

Masaryk in England

When the war broke out in August 1914 Masaryk, who had long foreseen the bursting of the storm and had 'dreaded the final decision' which would then be forced upon him—the conflict of loyalties, to the Czech nation and to the Austrian state—was 'in a state of constant tension', but at first avoided all expression of opinion and adopted a waiting attitude. This was perhaps the solitary advantage accruing to him from the fact that the Austrian Parliament was not allowed to meet at this supreme crisis, and that its members were thus almost as effectually muzzled as the rest of the nation. On the other hand, he possessed the immunities of a deputy, and hence the possibility of crossing the frontiers of the state: and this he used in September, in order to accompany his American sister-in-law to her steamer at Rotterdam, where he hoped to establish contact with his friends in the West.

He had in the meantime sent verbal messages to Mr Wickham Steed, then foreign editor of *The Times*, with whom he had become intimate during Steed's eleven years as correspondent in Vienna. Steed in his memoirs* gives a picturesque account of the messenger. 'One afternoon, towards the middle of September, when I was about to leave my house, I found a strange-looking man standing on the threshold. Thickset, of medium height, unshaven, grimy in appearance and in dress, with features of the semi-Tartar type that is not uncommon in Bohemia, he seemed an unprepossessing fellow.

"Are you Mr Steed?" he asked, with a strong foreign accent and a pronounced American intonation.

"Yes", I answered. "Who are you?"

"I'm Voska", he answered.

"I don't know you", I said. "What do you want?"

* *Through Thirty Years*, II, p. 42.

"I have a message from the Professor."

"What Professor?"

"Masaryk."

"Come in."

Voska came in and began: "I'm Voska, the head of the Bohemian Alliance in America. I am an American citizen."

"Where do you come from and when did you see the Professor?"

"I left Prague with thirty American citizens five days ago. In an hour I must catch my train to Liverpool with them. Before I left, the Professor said to me: 'In London see Mr Steed. Tell him the Russians shoot at our boys when they want to surrender. Our boys wave handkerchiefs, but the Russians shoot all the same. Tell Mr Steed to find means of stopping it. Our boys want to go over to the Russians.'"

"How on earth am I to stop it?" I asked. "Did Masaryk say nothing else?"

"No, that was all. He just said, 'Tell Mr Steed to stop it'."'

Voska was an American Czech of advanced political views, who had made a small fortune in a Kansas marble quarry, and had been on a visit to his native land when war broke out. The sequel to this message was Steed's warning to Masaryk, delivered verbally by a little Czech hunchback, who as a non-combatant was not prevented from returning to Prague. 'Find Professor Masaryk', the message ran. 'When you are alone with him, but not before, say: "Steed says the boys must sing Hej Slovaní at midnight." Forget this till you are alone with him, and forget it afterwards.' The other end of the story was a cipher message of the Russian Ambassador Count Benckendorff, duly instructed by Steed, to the Russian Foreign Minister Mr Sazonov, requesting that regimental commanders on the Russo-Austrian front should be instructed to listen at midnight for the singing of the Panslav hymn Hej Slované, or that other famous Slav song 'Poland is not yet lost'. This would mean that Czech or Slovak soldiers from the Austrian lines were about to come over to the Russians, and must not be fired upon. And thus began those wholesale surrenders which, two years later, rendered possible the formation of the famous Czechoslovak Legions in Russia.

At this point I ought perhaps to explain how I came to know Masaryk. Between 1905 and 1914 I had spent considerable portions of each year in the Habsburg Monarchy, making Vienna the centre of my studies and of constant travel in the Danubian and Balkan countries. I first met Professor Masaryk in 1910, in company with his friend and Maecenas, Charles R. Crane, at the house of Reuter's correspondent, Robert Atter and his American wife. I liked him, but for some years saw very little of him: there was a natural reserve about him which was never repellent, but did not make for speedy intimacy, especially with a man thirty years his junior. Moreover, in those years I happened to be really intimate with the Slovak poet Hurban Vajanský, who as an ardent Panslav warned me against Masaryk's realist attitude towards 'Holy Russia', and who also misjudged Masaryk's motives in defending that militant anti-Clerical, Professor Wahrmund. What gradually brought us together was his splendid attitude in the Southern Slav question. I was already behind the scenes of the Zagreb Treason Trial, and was thus able to test on the spot the most contentious points in his famous parliamentary defence of the Zagreb victims. At the Friedjung libel action I heard him give evidence on behalf of the Serbo-Croat Coalition, and my conversion to his views was completed by his political duel with the Foreign Minister Count Aehrenthal at the Austrian Delegation. I sent him my book on the Southern Slav Question, which appeared in the autumn of 1911, and on my return to Vienna after several months of Balkan travel during the wars of 1913, he was naturally the first man to whom I went with my experiences. When, then, in June 1914 I undertook a journey to Central Europe in order to win support for a new quarterly 'European Review', which I proposed founding—to be devoted to the study of all questions of nationality in Europe—I again turned naturally to him: and he and another prominent Czech politician, Dr Fiedler, drafted a special memorandum for private circulation, commending my project to the Czech public. (I had already enlisted many expert helpers in Berlin, Dresden, Vienna, Budapest and Cracow.)

The above brief summary should suffice to show why Masaryk's first overture was to Steed and myself.

During the opening weeks of the war I was actively engaged in organising practical help for Serbia, whose links with this country were then few and far between. I became Hon. Secretary of the Serbian Relief Fund, which in four years of war was destined to collect and distribute over £1,000,000 worth of material for sick and wounded and refugees: and at the same time I rapidly drifted into the position of an informal liaison officer between our people and the various exiled Slavs who turned to London for help and sympathy. Of these the first to arrive, and one of the most notable, was Frano Supilo, of whom Masaryk had declared in his evidence at the Friedjung Trial that he was ready to put his right hand in the fire for him and some of his colleagues. On three successive days in September *The Times* printed letters, written quite independently of each other, by Sir Valentine Chirol (whom Steed had recently succeeded as foreign editor), George Trevelyan and myself, intended to bring home to an uninformed public some of the main issues involved in the so-called 'Question of Nationalities' in Central Europe.

The result was that on 21 September I received a letter with a Dutch stamp, very inadequately addressed to me as 'Author of works on the Southern Slavs, etc., c/o Constable, Editor [a mistake for 'publisher'], London', and written at the Hotel Weimar in Rotterdam on the 17th by Professor Masaryk.

I—Masaryk to Seton Watson

"*Rotterdam, Hotel Weimar, 17. 9. 14.*

Dear Mr Seton-Watson,

I just was thinking about you when I found your letter to *The Times* (Southern Slav Patriotism). I was going to write to you, because I fear Mr Steed, to whom I wrote on the 14th, is not in London.

I came here to communicate with Mr Steed: I asked him to come here or to send you or somebody who could grasp the full meaning of what I would have to say now.

Bohemia (and Austria) is utterly quarantined—we read only what is allowed to be printed: of course we know how to read these official news. At any rate, I would like to hear what is going on, not only on the battlefields, but in the heads of those who will shape the future, perhaps the future map of Europe, at least of Austria. I wish that we Bohemians could say what we feel and what we hope.

I know how little knowledge of Austria the official world of Russia has, therefore I wish I could come in contact with this world through Mr Steed and his friends.

I can stay here until Monday (incl.) the 21st. Tuesday 22nd I will leave for Amsterdam, stay there the day and leave for Prague the 23rd. Therefore I could get news from England in Amsterdam also, Hotel Royal. Please tell Mr Steed that, and what I wrote him; telegraph me here whether you have got my letter and whether I can expect somebody from England here, *now*.

In the case that I could not see Mr Steed or somebody now, I am willing to come later. I would come from Prague: in that case send a telegram through some of the English correspondents or other persons living here in Holland.

The telegram 'Waldemar only wounded', sent from Holland, would reach me in Prague, and I would come to Rotterdam expecting to find a *poste restante* letter telling more about our communication.

This letter may be sent, A. R. Mill, Rotterdam, Poste Restante.

Should Mr Steed (you, etc.) prefer to communicate with me in Rome, I will come to Rome: in that case I expect a telegram 'Waldemar heavily* wounded', and I expect a letter in Rome

* He means 'badly' or 'severely'.

(again A. R. Mill), *ferma in poste*. Rome would give me the opportunity to see some of the Serbians and Russians: I wrote about that to Mr Steed.

Here [i.e. at the Hague], I would not dare to speak to the members of the Embassies: I must take care not to be followed by the Austrian spy too closely. In Rome—Naples—at Capri, I can move more freely. Of course I can come here, and later to Rome also.

You will understand that I cannot stay here too long; therefore I would have to come the second time.

I imagine I could come here in 2–3 weeks.

Yours sincerely, PROFESSOR MASARYK."

* * *

Fortunately this letter reached me safely: but it had been opened and detained for four days by the censor, and when I received it it was already too late to catch him at the Amsterdam address which he had given me. In actual fact he left Holland for Prague on the 23rd without having succeeded in establishing contact with any of his friends in the West.

For three weeks there was silence: and then came a message through *The Times* correspondent at the Hague to Mr Steed begging him to come over to Rotterdam, or to send a substitute. As it was obviously impossible for the foreign editor to leave London even for a day, he begged me to take his place. By a fortunate accident I was enabled to enter Holland without ever showing my passport, and this may explain the fact, which I ascertained in due course, that my meeting with Masaryk remained entirely unknown to the Austrian police agents in Holland.

We spent two days together, keeping mainly to our rooms for the day, and walking for miles along the quays after it was dark. I took detailed notes of our conversation and immediately on my return to England drew up a memorandum* embodying Masaryk's

* Printed here on pp. 40 ff.

ideas, not only as to the internal situation in Bohemia and in Austria-Hungary as a whole, but as to the settlement which ought to follow the war, and the policy which the Allies should pursue. It remained ultra-secret: I typed it out in four copies, keeping one for myself, giving one to Mr Steed, who transmitted it to the French Foreign Minister M. Delcassé, one to the Foreign Office, and a little later one to Professor Paul Vinogradoff of Oxford, who took it with him to Russia and handed it himself to the Russian Foreign Minister Mr Sazonov.* I also showed it to my two intimate collaborators Ronald Burrows, Principal of King's College, London, and A. F. (now Sir Frederick) Whyte. As a further precaution the name of Masaryk was not mentioned in the memorandum, but merely communicated verbally. I cannot resist adding—for the benefit of some foreign publicists and pamphleteers who have constructed fabulous tales of British pre-war designs and political agents—that until the occasion when I brought this memorandum to Mr George Clerk (for whom fate reserved the post of first British Minister in Prague), I had never once crossed the threshold of our Foreign Office, or had any relations whatsoever with any of its members. It was Steed who introduced me to Clerk, who was quick to realise the importance of Masaryk's memorandum, supplemented as it was by still more secret information about submarines and plans of mobilisation, and who from that time onwards was a sympathetic listener on all such subjects, and always ready to lay matters of urgency before his chief, Sir Edward Grey.

The memorandum speaks for itself: it provides eloquent proof of Masaryk's far-seeing statesmanship.

* Mr Lowrie, in his short biography, *Masaryk of Czechoslovakia* (p. 164), says that I 'came with the consent of the British Government to discuss war-plans', and that I 'sent a special memorandum to the Russian Tsar'. Both statements are quite imaginary.

MEMORANDUM ON CONVERSATIONS WITH MASARYK

(October 1914)

My informant prefaced his remarks by a personal anecdote, as characteristic of the whole situation in Bohemia. On returning from his first visit to Holland, at the end of September, he found an official notice waiting for him, to the effect: 'Your newspaper is in every way "illoyal". One more confiscation, and it will be suppressed altogether.' Knowing this notice to have come directly from the Governor of Bohemia, Prince Thun, he obtained a private interview with the latter and discussed the whole situation with him with great frankness.

Two or three days before their meeting the 28th regiment, belonging to the city of Prague, left for the front in Galicia, and on its departure both the soldiers and the general public showed their Slav sentiments in a very marked way; not merely was 'Hej Slovaní' sung with the greatest enthusiasm, including the verse 'Rus je s nami' (the Russian is with us), but a white flag was actually carried before the regiment, on which an extra verse was inscribed to the effect that 'we are marching against the Russians, but nobody knows why!' This the authorities did not dare to remove, or to indulge in any reprisals against the crowd. Prince Thun sent a confidential report to Vienna regarding the whole incident, and my informant had found means to learn the contents of this report through a trustworthy source, and thus knew Thun's attitude, and was able to contrast it with any possible expressions of opinion during their conversation.

He therefore spoke quite openly to Thun. His remarks may be summed up under the following heads:

(1) All Czech parties without exception have the Slav programme and Slav sentiments. The nation is Russophil and Serbophil, and this fact cannot be changed.

(2) But above all it is anti-Prussian. You (Prince Thun) and your party (the Catholic Conservatives and the 'Grossgrundbesitz') may very soon need the help of this feeling, as you fall more and more into the toils of Berlin.

(3) The Germans of Prague are very aggressive and excited, and as they are mainly Jews, the anti-Semite feeling is growing more acute. It is essential that you (Thun) should hold back the Jews and render them less aggressive ('herausfordernd'); otherwise there might be a Jewish Pogrom, and that would only be the beginning, and would be infinitely regrettable.

(4) The reports from the Hauptquartier are so crassly stupid that every child sees through them; and they thus tend to foster anti-Austrian feeling.

(5) Prague sees thousands and thousands of wounded soldiers, who all say that Austria was not prepared, and that there were no proper sanitary or commissariat arrangements.

In short, it is impossible for us Czechs to feel as you would like us to feel; that is a fact which must be faced. And now you can do with me and my paper what you like! To all this Thun made no answer at all, except to say that it interested him extremely. But since then my informant's paper has had considerably more latitude, and though confiscated has not been suppressed.

This interview sums up the feeling of all Bohemia. On the outbreak of war every effort was made to induce the Czech parties to follow the example of the Polish Club in the Galician Diet, the Germans of Vienna and Bohemia, and the Slovene Clerical People's Party under Dr Šusteršić, in issuing Austrophil declarations. Not a single party consented. *Hlas Naroda*, the Old Czech organ, writes against Russia, but even it does not represent the true feeling of the Old Czech party, which may be less pronouncedly Russophil, but is none the less Russophil. No other newspaper is even remotely anti-Russian, though of course none are free to write in favour of Russia.

The reports of rioting circulated in the foreign press are incorrect. There have been no disturbances of any kind, and no executions except for military insubordination. The only Czech leader in prison is Mr Klofáč. My informant was able to learn the contents of the police report on Klofáč's arrest. It is based on alleged anarchism (certain intercepted letters addressed to him from persons of anarchic views in Switzerland) and on the further allegation that he had submitted his speeches in the Austrian Delegation to the Serbian Government's approval before they were delivered.

It is utterly impossible for Bohemia to move until the Russians arrive, but it is hardly an exaggeration to assert that the state of feeling is so unanimous in favour of the Allies that even Czechs in the pay of the police really privately sympathise with Russia.

My informant was unable to describe himself definitely as a mandatory, our meeting being intended rather as a scouting expedition to prepare the ground. He has now returned and will take further and more definite action, to be defined later on. As soon, however, as the situation permits, he desires to come over to England and to France, with the object of getting into personal touch with the two Allied Governments and with the Russian ambassadors in Bordeaux and London, as soon as he has been able to consult all those whose co-operation is essential.

In the meantime, though not a mandatory in so many words, he had actually spoken, before his first visit to Holland, to leaders of the Socialist, Constitutional (Dr Hajn) and National Socialist parties and, though not with Dr Kramář himself, with certain other Young Czechs—with the result that he feels himself to be speaking for all these four parties as well as for his own followers —in all that I am now about to summarise as the result of our conversations.

Hitherto, there have been three meetings of the leaders of the Czech parties, but for mainly technical reasons, such as the discussion of relief, administration, etc.

In broad outlines, the following forecast of Bohemia's future, as my informant would like to see it, is certain of the approval of all middle-class parties and of the nation at large and of the entire younger generation. Opposition to it need only be expected from (1) the aristocracy, which will be openly loyal to the Emperor, almost without exception, and is not likely to throw in its lot with the new State, and from (2) the Clericals, a section of whom will intrigue against such a solution, but less openly, trying to undermine the solidarity of the nation by indirect tactics. But even here some Russophil tendencies will manifest themselves; and it is in this connection, as in Poland, that Russian Orthodoxy will require to show considerable restraint and tact in its relations to Catholicism in Bohemia and elsewhere. (This last sentence does not represent the *ipsissima verba* of my informant, but more his half-suggested opinion, which is the more valuable as coming from an open opponent of Austrian Clericalism.)

THE FUTURE OF BOHEMIA

My informant was careful to emphasise at the outset that an independent Bohemia such as he desires represents a *maximum* programme, and is absolutely inconceivable unless and until Germany is crushed. The younger generation believes firmly in the possibility of this maximum. The pamphlets widely circulated in Bohemia in the middle of October—in the form of a manifesto of the Tsar to the Bohemian nation—are quite symptomatic. They are alleged to have been dropped from a Russian aeroplane, but in reality were secretly printed in Prague. It is also known in Bohemia that on the occasion of the Tsar's visit to Moscow, three Czech residents there had an audience with him and openly expressed the hope that Bohemia would be liberated at his hands.

He emphasised the fact that Bohemia is the key to the situation and that the Austro-Hungarian and German armies will resist to the uttermost in the district surrounding Cracow, for many reasons, political and economic. Their supplies of coal, iron and salt depend upon holding it. A decisive blow can be dealt at Prussia in one of two ways—either directly or through Austria. To weaken or crush Austria-Hungary is the effectual way of weakening Germany. Bismarck's whole policy was based upon the attempt to prevent this theory from being put into practice; and even his successors, in spite of their inept diplomacy, are well aware of Bohemia's strategic importance. For Russia, the occupation of Vienna or Budapest is the show, the occupation of Prague is the reality; they will stay longer in Vienna if they take Prague first. They must, however, on no account enter Bohemia except to stay: or the consequences might be absolutely fatal. It is certain that the same policy would be adopted afterwards as in Syrmia, where the Austro-Hungarian authorities have systematically wiped out all the villages which had welcomed the Serbs. Russia must at all costs avoid a mere policy of 'raids', such as that to Mármaros Sziget last month.

Without a decisive defeat of Germany there can be no independent Bohemia; but, Germany once defeated, it can be created on maximum lines. In that case the proper course would be to restore the historical Bohemia-Moravia-Silesia, and to add to this the Slovak districts of Hungary (Slovensko). The southern frontier of the new State would then follow the boundary between the existing provinces of Bohemia-Moravia and Upper-Lower Austria, though certain slight modifications could be made to the south-west of Budweis and between Gmünd and Znajm, on an ethnographical basis. The boundary would then follow the river March to its mouth in the Danube, then the line of the Danube itself, north of the Schütt, as far as the mouth of the river Eipel. It would then follow the course of the Eipel to near its source, and then as closely as possible the ethnographical boundary between Slovaks and Magyars, and later between Slovaks and Ruthenes. It would thus include Pressburg (Bratislava) and Kaschau (Košice), but Tokay and its vineyards would remain in Hungary, while Ungvár (Užhorod), Munkács (Mukačevo) and Mármaros Sziget would be incorporated in the Russian Empire.

In his opinion the new State could only be a kingdom, not a republic; a decided majority of the nation would favour this. In the interest of its future, and above all in the interest of the future of Russo-Bohemian relations—this he strongly emphasised—it would be wiser not to place a Russian Grand Duke on the throne, but rather a Western prince, preferably a Dane or a Belgian. He is of opinion that in that event the intimacy with Russia is more likely to subsist—paradoxical as it may seem at first sight—than in the event of a direct Russian sovereignty, which would tend merely to bring out the difference of outlook. The selection of a sovereign is, moreover, one of quite special importance, if the *historic* kingdom is to be restored; for there would then be an important minority of 3-4,000,000 Germans, who would accept a Danish, but never a Russian, prince. In this connection it is to be observed that the Germans of Bohemia to-day look towards Berlin, but will cease to do so if the power of Prussia has once been crushed; while the Czech minorities in the northern German districts of Bohemia will at once raise their heads under the new regime. A tactful and moderate administration, under a carefully selected prince, leaving proper latitude to the schools and institutions of the Germans, but at the same time actively encouraging these Czech minorities, ought to produce a consolidated Bohemia long before Berlin could again, if ever, become threatening.

Such a new State will have two new neighbours—autonomous Poland and Russia herself; and for the success of the scheme it is essential that Russia should directly border upon Bohemia. It can, however, only be achieved if the Russian army occupies the whole territory in question, and holds it long enough to enable the preliminary organisation to be carried out. The economic and administrative sides of the problem are really thornier than the political, which depends above all upon the success of the Russian armies. It is on economic grounds that my informant bases his chief argument for including the German districts in North Bohemia, on the one hand owing to the fact that these districts contain the industrial centres without which Bohemia could not be self-supporting, and on the other hand because it will be necessary for the new State to take over a considerable part of

Austria's debts, and in that case it can less than ever afford to lose some of the wealthiest districts of the country, the more so as, wherever the frontier may be drawn, economic conditions are certain to continue the steady influx of Czech minorities into the northern districts of Bohemia.

It would be necessary for Bohemia—following the precedent of Hungary in 1867—to take over a portion of the Austrian debt which, it is calculated, will amount, after the war expenses have been added to the existing debt, to 30 milliards of crowns (kronen). Of this, at least six milliards would fall to the share of Bohemia-Moravia-Silesia; but as it would probably be necessary to pay extra for full freedom, the sum may be reckoned at 9 or 10 milliards in round figures. My informant, with the help of expert financial opinion, is engaged in making the necessary detailed calculations, which will be accessible if the right time arrives.

Bohemia's assets would fall under the following heads: (1) existing taxes; (2) coal-mines (the new State could make some arrangement such as would assure it a definite income from this source), graphite, sugar, and the textile industry; (3) electricity is capable of great developments; (4) real estate—*Grossgrundbesitz* and *Fideicommiss* (entailed estates). The State would almost certainly have to buy over large tracts from the present aristocracy, which would for the most part elect to remain in Vienna.

Informed opinion in Bohemia would unquestionably favour the adoption of the franc, as the currency would then be suitable both for the West and for Russia (40 francs = 15 roubles).

It is suggested that to ease the financial situation at the outset, the enormous enthusiasm which the creation of an independent Bohemia would evoke might be used to impose a kind of income tax (*Vermögensteuer*) similar to that imposed by the German Reichstag. This would avoid making fresh debts at the very beginning, and is the sort of step which might arouse far more opposition at a later stage.

In the event of a Russian occupation of Prague, the invaders would presumably summon some of the Czech leaders as their advisers. The obvious persons for this task would be: Dr Kramář for the Young Czechs; Mr Švehla for the Agrarians; Mr Klofáč or Mr Choc for the National Socialists; Professor Masaryk for the Realists.

My informant urges very strongly that the Russians, if and when they are able to invade Bohemia (this would apply even more strongly to the Slovak country—R. W. S.-W.), should not attempt to form the proposed Bohemian or 'Hussite' Legion, on the lines of the Polish Legion. They would be well advised to wait till a slightly later stage, and as soon as they are actually in Bohemia should employ the Sokol organisation for the purpose of keeping order. The Sokols would thus become a kind of militia or Gardes Civiques, and thus the nucleus of the future Bohemian army. He has already discussed such an idea with some of their more serious members, and found them favourable. He intends discussing the matter with their chief on returning home just now. A further advantage is that they have considerable money resources, which are in safe hands and can be employed whenever required.

Note. His arguments in favour of the *historic* Bohemia-Moravia-Silesia plus the Slovak districts, as opposed to a new Czecho-Slovak *racial* State, rest on the extreme difficulty of drawing a tenable frontier on a basis of ethnography. If, however, the arguments in favour of an ethnographic frontier should prevail at the settlement, he submits that concessions should be made on the south-west of Bohemia towards Upper Austria and in Silesia, the German portion of which could be united to German Silesia, while the Polish portion, like the Polish portion of the latter, fell to the new autonomous Russian Poland. Northern Bohemia, however, he argues is essential to the existence and prosperity of the new State, both from the economic standpoint and in the interests of the Czech racial minorities.

R. W. Seton-Watson.

* * *

Our conversations naturally ranged over many other subjects which lay outside the scope of the above memorandum. But instead of attempting to reproduce them after the lapse of twenty-seven years, I prefer to give my rough notes, as they were written down at the time, and recovered the other day from a mislaid dossier.

Points re England

"(1) *As principle:*

The role of Britain in the future settlement should be 'the Brain policy'. She should have a plan, and the European public ought to know it. This will (1) give direction to the evolution of events and (2) win the sympathies of Europe. This ought to come *now*.

(2) *Wishes:*

(*a*) Britain should send to France as many soldiers as possible, as soon as possible. Masaryk is afraid that France may not be able to hold out alone.

(*b*) *The Times* of 16 September contains a statement of Sazonov saying that Russia had hitherto bought everything from Germany, and urging that British experts should be sent to Russia even during the war. This is not enough. Russia should be induced by Britain to make a provisional treaty with Britain, France and Belgium, to the effect that Russia will not buy from Germany. This would have a great tactical effect, it would deal a blow to Germany, and would secure us in the future. It would give a direction, a lead, to the Russian people.

(*c*) Universal service, on Swiss lines, should be introduced.

(*d*) There should be a military convention of the Western States—Britain, France, Belgium, Denmark and perhaps Holland (this would be roughly $45+40+7+8=100$ versus 65 millions). France alone can never stand against Germany. United under British leadership, we could then hold our own, even without Russia. He does not expect any positive effect in the direction of democratisation.

(*e*) Holland might perhaps be induced to join in. But he feared lest it might prove impossible to secure the restoration of Belgium. If the final settlement followed purely ethnographic lines, was there not a danger of Belgium being divided between France and Holland? Would the religious problem militate against reaction? Would division offer a better chance of financial recuperation? (On this point alone Masaryk showed hesitation and uncertainty: it was doubtless the problem on which he had least personal knowledge.)

(*f*) There must be an understanding with Russia. To-day the position was as it were purely accidental ('eine Zufallsposition'). It must be regularised. And this involved a clear agreement with France and Italy.

(*g*) There must be a Quadruple Entente, including Italy.

(*h*) As to Greater Britain, he showed himself fully alive to the vital role of the Dominions.

(*i*) Among the internal reforms of Britain itself, which seemed to him to be necessary, were a reorganisation of the chemical industry and improvement in the production of torpedoes (the German brand being, according to his military informants in Austria, superior to the British)."

* * *

These penetrating criticisms of the whole wide field of military and political warfare were of course merely in the nature of an entirely informal preliminary survey, and I felt that it would be wiser to keep them to myself. They were to bear fruit eighteen months later in his Memorandum 'At the Eleventh Hour' (see p. 153).

Needless to say, Balkan problems figured prominently in our conversations. Among other information which Masaryk asked me to communicate to the proper authority in London were certain facts with regard to the Roumanian situation which he had obtained from secret informants inside the War Ministry in Vienna. The most important point was that on 25–27 September 1914 a meeting took place at Kronstadt (Braşov in Transylvania) between two Austrian agents—G. Freitag (probably an assumed name) and T. Jonescu Canaan, a Roumanian subject, and Madame Math. Sturdza, wife of Lieutenant Conrad Sturdza, adjutant to General Lambrino of the Corps Commando in Jassy. This lady, acting for her husband, handed over the Roumanian plan of mobilisation—a document of 32 pages. It was arranged that at the commencement of the actual mobilisation, to which the document provided the key, a telegram should be sent containing the words 'Je vous félicite'. The price paid was 4000 Kronen (£165). This report reached the Ballplatz not later than 13 October.

On reaching London I of course communicated this without delay to the Foreign Office, and Mr Clerk told me that the information had been sent to Sir George Barclay, our Minister in Bucarest, leaving it to his discretion as to how the Roumanians should be informed of this act of treachery. I did not communicate it to M. Mişu, the Roumanian Minister in London, because it was obviously necessary to cover up as far as possible the source of information. During my first conversation with Sir George Barclay at Bucarest, at the end of January 1915, I naturally alluded to this incident, adding that I was now at liberty to reveal the source, as Masaryk had escaped from Austria and burnt his boats. At the moment the Minister showed little or no interest in the matter, but I afterwards learnt that I had scarcely left the room before he sent for the Military Attaché, Colonel Napier, and asked him his opinion of the document in question, which he had kept beside him unused for over two months. Colonel Napier, realising at once the importance of the matter, asked and obtained the Minister's permission to communicate the facts without delay to the Minister of War. Next day he himself told me what transpired. Soon after three o'clock that afternoon he called at the General Staff and was received with great courtesy; he was puzzled to find that the information caused neither surprise nor consternation, but was dismissed smilingly, and almost casually. On returning to his hotel, Napier met his Russian colleague and thought it wise to inform him. The Russian was much excited and provided the explanation. He had himself received only that morning a cipher from Rome containing the same facts, and had communicated them to the same Staff Officer in the afternoon, leaving him barely a quarter of an hour before Napier arrived. I afterwards discovered that Masaryk had informed the Russian Embassy in Rome, though of course assuming that the facts had long ago reached Bucarest. The real point of the story lies in the fact that this same Sturdza was later guilty of treasonable relations with the Germans at a critical moment during Mackensen's invasion of Roumania, and indeed fled to the camp of the invader. If events had moved in the direction of Roumania's entry into the war in 1915—as was at one time by no means impossible—the betrayal of this document might have had fatal results. As it was, the General Staff presumably issued new mobilisation orders, but the traitor, belonging as he did to one of the foremost families of Roumania, would appear to have been left untouched.

Fate had thus made of me the first intermediary between Masaryk and the Entente. I also carried with me and posted in London a letter for M. Ernest Denis, supplementing one which had already been posted direct from Holland. Denis was Professor at the Sorbonne, author of the classical history of Bohemia*—a man of high character and great charm, belonging to a leading Calvinist family and perhaps the most eminent of a small band of French Slavophil intellectuals. M. Denis, not knowing where to send his reply to Masaryk, posted it to me in London, and I too did not dare to send it on, with the result that it reached Masaryk's hands only after his arrival in London in April 1915: but

* *La Fin de l'Indépendance Tchèque*, and *La Bohême depuis la Montagne Blanche*: he was also author of books on modern German history, and during the war published three volumes entitled *La Grande Serbie*, *Les Slovaques* and *La Guerre*.

Denis's covering letter to me is of great interest, for it outlines his original ideas for an European settlement on national lines, and it therefore belongs to this correspondence.*

II—Ernest Denis to R. W. Seton-Watson

"Cher Monsieur,

J'avais reçu il y a quelques jours une première lettre de M. Masaryk, et sur sa demande je lui osais aussitôt télégraphier à Rotterdam. Ma dépêche semble ne pas être arrivée à temps.

La nouvelle lettre que vous avez eu la bonté de me transmettre, me dit seulement qu'il a l'intention de revenir en France dans quelque temps, et qu'il demande de lui faciliter ici le séjour, en écartant les objections qui pourraient naître de sa qualité de sujet austro-hongrois.

Je viens d'écrire au Ministre des Affaires Étrangères, et j'espère que nous obtiendrons tous les sauf-conduits nécessaires. Dès que j'aurai une réponse je vous la transmettrai de manière à éviter les pertes de temps. Il va sans dire que je serai très heureux de recevoir M. Supilo et de causer avec lui.

La question de l'Autriche-Hongrie me paraît assez difficile à résoudre. Voici les idées qui me sont venues.

Établir une confédération assez large, de manière à laisser à chaque diète une autorité fort étendue: n'accorder au Parlement centrale que l'autorité nécessaire pour les affaires militaires et étrangères, les chemins de fer et les postes.

Comme il sera toujours impossible de suivre exactement les limites ethnographiques, établir par des lois constitutionnelles des garanties absolues pour les minorités; égalité absolue des langues, écoles et universités; supprimer tout ce qui peut ressembler à la domination d'une race sur l'autre; liberté religieuse complète; liberté de la presse et des associations.

La Transylvanie relâchée à la Roumanie.

* I published it in *Le Monde Slave* for May 1930.

La Bosnie, l'Herzégovine, la Dalmatie, une partie de la Croatie rattachée à la Serbie, et par conséquent exclue de l'Autriche.

La confédération autrichienne se composera de quatre parties:

(1) Bohême, Moravie, Silésie, Slovaquie.
(2) Provinces allemandes.
(3) Hongrie, réduite aux pays réellement magyares.
(4) Groupe yougoslave (Carniole, Sud de la Carinthie, partie de la Styrie, partie de la Croatie). Trieste fera part de ce groupe, mais sera port franc.

La Roumanie accrue de la Transylvanie et d'une partie de la Bucovine, abandonnera à la Bulgarie la rive droite du Danube: la Bulgarie recevra de plus Andrinople et s'il est possible Cavala; la Serbie abandonnera sur la rive gauche du Vardar les territoires bulgares qu'elle a du temps de la dernière guerre.

La Grèce en dehors de Cavala obtiendra l'Épire du sud. L'Italie recevra le Trentin italien et Valona.

Naturellement tout ceci est très schématique: il faut tenir compte d'intérêts très divers et de considérations multiples. Mais avec de la bonne volonté il n'est pas impossible, semble-t-il, de créer une situation tolérable. Les haines ethniques s'éteindront du jour où les exigences les plus essentielles seront satisfaites et où l'oppression disparaîtra partout.

Agréez, Monsieur, l'assurance de mes sentiments les plus dévoués, le 31 Octobre 1914.

ERNEST DENIS.

Je vous envoie à tout hasard une lettre pour M. Masaryk, dans le cas où vous pourriez le lui faire parvenir."

III—ERNEST DENIS TO T. G. MASARYK

"Mon cher Collègue,

M. Seton-Watson m'envoie votre lettre du 25 Octobre. J'avais reçu déjà le 27 votre lettre de Rotterdam, dans laquelle vous me priez de vous télégraphier: Lettre Reçue. J'ai naturellement télégraphié aussitôt. Je ne sais pas si mon télégramme vous est parvenu.

Je viens immédiatement d'écrire au Ministère des Affaires Étrangères et j'espère obtenir le sauf-conduit que vous désirez. Dès que j'aurai une réponse, je préviendrai M. Seton-Watson. Il va sans dire que je serais très heureux de causer avec vous et que je me mets à votre entière disposition pour tout ce qui pourrait vous être agréable où utile. Je serai toujours très heureux de pouvoir servir la cause de la Bohême, et je considère comme devoir de consacrer mes dernières forces à préparer à l'Europe un neilleur avenir.

Croyez, mon cher collègue, à mes sentiments affectueux,

le 31 Octobre 1914. ERNEST DENIS."

* * *

After Masaryk's return to Prague no further communications between us were possible, though occasionally American Czechs, passing homewards from Prague, brought verbal messages. One of his first steps was to discuss the foreign situation with some of his Prague colleagues, and to ask for their verbal sanction for the work to be done abroad. 'This was because of Seton-Watson's hint that politicians in Allied countries would want to know if I was speaking and acting in my own name, or in that of our political parties, and if so, which parties.' From the very first there was a strong current among the Czechs—led by the 'Young Czech' leader Dr Karel Kramář—in favour of complete political passivity and reliance upon a Russian invasion, in which event a Russian Grand Duke might become King of Bohemia. Masaryk was too good a democrat to feel much enthusiasm for the Romanov dynasty, and his realism, based upon prolonged and intimate study of Russian psychology and political thought, warned him that Russia alone would never be able to solve the problem of the Western Slav nations, much less to bring them liberty. But while the ultra-Russophils (all Czechs were Russophil up to a certain point) were depressed by the terrible reverses which followed upon the first victories of the Tsarist armies, Masaryk never lost his balance, and soon realised that the fate of his nation was bound up with that of the Western democracies and America, and also that a great educational and propagandist work would be required before the Western public could be expected to understand the Czech problem in its Austrian setting, and to accept the idea of active co-operation. In this connection the knowledge that Kitchener and other Western leaders were reckoning with a three-years' war materially influenced his whole political attitude: for it was obvious that not less than three years would be required to prepare the world for a programme of complete independence, whereas if the war should only last half that time a strong case might be put forward in favour of a much more modest programme of national autonomy inside the framework of the Habsburg Monarchy.

Masaryk left Austria for the third and last time on 18 December, this time for Rome, without of course being able to inform us of his plans; and thus it came about that George Trevelyan and I, who started from London on the 15th for Serbia and Roumania (with the double purpose of studying the practical side of hospital assistance to the Serbs and exploring the possibilities of Roumanian intervention), left Rome on the eve of his arrival there. During our brief stay, however, we established contact with Trumbić, Meštrović, Lujo Vojnović and several other prominent Jugoslav refugees from Dalmatia, who in the first period of the war found neutral Italy the most convenient rallying point. I told them of Supilo's activities in London and of my meeting with Masaryk, and prepared them for his arrival in Rome. On our return two months later I found that he had at once got into touch with them, and had even used their good offices at the Russian Embassy; and it seems to have been this which drew upon him the suspicions of the Austro-Hungarian authorities, who were already keeping close watch upon the Jugoslav exiles in neutral countries. In his memoirs Masaryk tells us that he 'envied the Jugoslavs for having so many political men abroad', but soon came to realise that there were fruitful causes of dissension among them, and in sober fact one of the great assets of the Czechoslovak movement proved to be his own position, head and shoulders above all his colleagues in exile.

After about a month's stay he was on the point of returning home for the third time, but in the nick of time warnings arrived from Beneš in Prague and from the poet Machar in Vienna—on the basis of confidential information from an unknown friend inside the Austrian Ministry of War—that he would be arrested as soon as he set foot on Austrian soil, and probably summarily executed. On 11 January he left Rome for Geneva and settled there until the necessary passport arrangements could be made for his visit to Paris and London. On my way back from the Balkans in the second week of February I found a postcard awaiting me at my hotel in Rome: 'Hotel Richmond, Geneva, 6.2.15. If your way home would allow you to stop in Geneva (I presume you go over Paris) please do so. I would be very glad to see you here. Yours, Prof. Masaryk.'

We spent a whole day together in Geneva, exchanging information and laying plans for his proposed visit to the West. This was immediately after his first Swiss meeting with Dr Beneš, who then returned to Prague with Masaryk's messages for the Maffia, as the innermost revolutionary organisation of the Czech movement now came to be called: their talks laid the first definite plans for a campaign abroad in favour of Czech independence.

In the end he was delayed rather longer than he had expected in Switzerland. Its central geographical position made it the best centre for a subterranean news service, and an ideal meeting-place in which men of many parties and nations could pool facts and ideas. He also had some reason to be critical of the weekly papers published by the small Czech colony in Paris, and it was essential for him, before he crossed the French frontier, to create in Geneva a reliable organisation, well versed in all the strange technique of

III. EDWARD BENEŠ (1921)

conspiracy and secret messages. He was also delayed by illness—it was on this occasion that he suffered from small abscesses on the shoulder, which his doctor ascribed to poisoning, 'and our own people thought the Germans were trying to get at me through my laundry'. Above all, there was the difficulty of obtaining a passport. Eventually the Serbian Government, mindful of his decisive role in the Zagreb and Friedjung trials, provided him with a diplomatic passport, in which every particular was accurate except the statement that he was a Serbian citizen. It was left to me to arrange the British visa, with the help of Mr Clerk and Mr Steed, but there was some delay with the necessary formalities, and on 5 March I received a telegram from Geneva—'Avez-vous oublié Consul. Nouvelles importantes. Masaryk.' This was followed by a letter, briefly announcing the tragic death of his son Herbert from typhus in South Bohemia. His own reaction, when anonymous enemies wrote to him of 'The Finger of God', was the simple phrase recorded in his memoirs: 'to me it seemed rather an injunction not to abate or to grow weary in my efforts.' Meanwhile he had got into touch with Count Francis Lützow, that *rara avis* among the Bohemian feudal nobility, who felt as a Czech patriot and had long been a pioneer of Hussite studies in English. Lützow, with his many English contacts, encouraged him to come to London, and fully endorsed his attitude to Russian and general Slav questions.

IV—Masaryk to Seton-Watson

20 March 1915

"Dear Mr Seton-Watson,

Mr Campbell came and we agreed to send my letters via Paris through *The Times* office.

In about a week Mr Kepl is coming to London: he will tell you all the literary and journalistic plans we agreed upon with Prof. Denis; he will also be able to arrange things in our Bohemian colony.

I will come to London, and I hope soon. I have some difficulties to get the necessary passport, and then I have to stay here with my surgeon, who takes care of a wound which I have acquired very unnecessarily.

I feel the awful war very intimately: my son died last Monday, the typhoid fever, caused and spread by the war, took him away. I could not go to Prague, as my friends sent very urgent warnings the very same day he died. They are threatening in Vienna with shooting (I infer from that, that some of my letters were intercepted). My younger son* is to be sent to the front, having had military training of eight weeks. You see I live the Bohemian question, but I agree with you that this question must be made known to those who don't know it.

Thank you for the news about my book:† about the other questions we can soon, I hope, speak in London.

Sincerely yours, T. G. MASARYK."

ADDENDUM TO IV

[In this letter were enclosed a number of notes and jottings in Masaryk's handwriting, which are worth including, as illustrations of his day-to-day method in exile.]

"A. *Socialists in Germany*. In Berlin the Liebknecht current is gaining strength among the Socialists. In Vienna too a growing opposition is noticeable against the *Arbeiterzeitung* current (Leuthner, Austerlitz).‡ Received from Berlin, 11th March. Liebknecht's latest speech in the Reichstag confirms this news: he would not dare to speak thus if he did not know the masses were for him.

B. *Austria. Italy*. In the south half a million soldiers are massed against Italy on the Austrian and German side ready to

* Jan Masaryk, afterwards Czechoslovak Minister in London till 1938 and Foreign Minister in the exiled Government in 1939.

† A reference to my suggestion for an English edition of *Russland und Europa*.

‡ Two of the chief editors of that paper.

march. If Italy misbehaves in the least degree they will march. Received 12 March. Vienna treats Italy as canaille. Vienna and Berlin think the Italians fear the Austrians, and still more the Germans. An offensive would frighten them to death.

C. *Austria. Italy. Trentino.* In the Crown Council the Emperor [Francis Joseph] expected that Conrad* would vote with him: but Conrad voted with the Ministers who were for the cession of the Trentino and a district as far as the Isonzo. Afterwards, in order to sweeten the bitter pill, it was argued that the cession was only temporary and academic, and that the victory of the Central Powers would restore Trentino and more still. The latter view is widespread in Vienna. This news came to me on 12th: the *Temps* of 15 March is not right in detail.

D. *Trentino.* The Emperor already once before, when Italy's attitude was discussed, coined the phrase 'Treachery is not paid for'. I hear this phrase from many sides.

E. *Losses.*

Germany—480,000 dead, 96,000 wounded, 232,000 prisoners.

Austria—341,000 dead, 80,000 wounded.

Received 12 March. The figures give the exact number. Austria has lost far more in prisoners, therefore the number is not given."

* * *

There was a special reason for our impatience at these delays. During April the secret negotiations between the Triple Entente and Italy were coming to a head, and culminated on 26 April 1915 in the Treaty of London, which recognised Italian claims not merely to the Trentino, Trieste and other Italian districts of Austria, but to Istria, a large part of Dalmatia, and a population of close upon a million Slovenes and Croats. Our friend Frano Supilo was by this time in Petrograd, and having worked the secret out of Sazonov himself, sent urgent cipher telegrams to Steed and myself through the medium of the Serbian Legation: and we in our turn were doing all in our power to hold back the authorities from making an agreement which we regarded as

* Marshal Conrad von Hötzendorf, Chief of General Staff.

mischievous in itself and only too likely to galvanise Austrian resistance by rallying the Southern Slav population in defence of Vienna. In this situation we naturally turned to Masaryk, whose authority in Southern Slav questions was hardly less than in those of his native Bohemia: and we hoped that he would strengthen the hands of the Croat and Serb leaders whose arrival we were awaiting, and at the same time help to enlighten the Foreign Office on the issues at stake. We therefore sent him the message—'Your presence highly desirable. Come soon, telegraphing route and hour of arrival.'

And so, on the evening of 18 April 1915, I met him and his daughter Olga at Charing Cross station. It was a rainy night, the station was dreary and unlit, there were no porters, and he and I had difficulty in dragging his heavy chest of books down the platform—a carefully selected armoury of weapons for the propaganda which he had come to wage. Then there were no taxis, and I can still see the two solitary figures standing guard over their luggage while I scoured the neighbouring streets for ten minutes before one of the rare taxis of those early war days could be found.

Masaryk immediately linked up with the tiny group of Czechophils who were at this time in the habit of meeting at the Czech Club in North London. The Czech colony was small and uninfluential, consisting mainly of tailors, furriers, waiters and hairdressers: its two most active members were Jan Sykora, who afterwards went back to run a restaurant at his native Pilsen, and F. Kopecky, a miniature painter, who after the war published a curious mystical novel. Among their English friends were Eugene Sully, who as secretary of the Physical Culture Society had learned to appreciate the great work of the Bohemian Sokols; Francis Marchant, a schoolmaster at Streatham; James Baker, author of a somewhat superficial book on Bohemia, who lived in Bristol and therefore could not often be present; a solicitor named Woodcock and a Congregational minister named Nicholson. That we were literally beginning at the letter A became apparent from the preliminary discussions as to the name of our society.

Should it be called 'Bohemian', or would that connect it in the eyes of an ignorant public with the activities of Prince Florizel and the Soho Suicide Club? And as for calling it 'Czech', who had ever heard the name, and would the public not pronounce it 'Zek'? And at this stage I intervened to point out that the Slovaks must not be ignored, and that there would be trouble if Czech and Slovak were not put upon an equal footing. In the end it was agreed that our little body should in the first instance be called 'Anglo-Czech Committee', and that any decision on the Slovak question should be postponed until Masaryk's arrival, and left to his decision. Needless to say he immediately endorsed my view as the only possible solution, but the question of a hyphen between Czech and Slovak was at first left open. Many a time in post-war Slovakia did I have occasion to tell the story of these discussions to cantankerous Slovaks who accused Masaryk and his friends of 'Czechisation'. Masaryk was of course himself a Slovak, but he combined in his own person to an unique degree the sentiments and outlook of the twin peoples, and from the first insisted on parity between them.

Owing to a curious accident I found myself the intermediary between Masaryk and the Foreign Office, and brought him to see Mr Clerk, who had already arranged for the permit which enabled him to cross the Channel. What I have called an accident was the extraordinary fact that Steed had incurred the wrath of Sir Edward Grey by criticising in *The Times* the manner in which our Ambassador in Constantinople had allowed himself to be fooled by the Turkish Government. From November 1914 till early in May 1915 access to the Foreign Office had been denied to him and his colleagues on the Thunderer: and the result was that from time to time I had to serve as go-between for certain matters concerning Austria. This awkward situation was complicated by the fact that Steed and I were the sole repositories of Supilo's warning from Petrograd, and felt bound to do what we could to prevent an unholy bargain being struck at the expense of one of those smaller nations of which there was so much sentimental talk. Sir Arthur Evans, the veteran of Southern Slav studies in this country, whom we initiated into the facts, wrote a long article in the *Manchester Guardian*, and I backed it up with a letter in *The Times*, but owing to the censorship it was not possible to tell the full facts, and needless to say there was never the slightest chance of our preventing the conclusion of the Treaty. When the authorities realised that we knew the essential facts about the Treaty of London, I was received by Grey, and Steed in Paris by Delcassé. While the former assured me that both the British and French military authorities had given it as their opinion that Italy's entry would decide the issue of the war, and that in such circumstances he, as a civilian Minister, could not take the grave responsibility of ignoring their advice, Delcassé on his side was less frank, and neither affirmed nor denied the Treaty's existence. But he admitted that 'Italy put a pistol at our heads', and argued that her entry, followed by that of Roumania, which he then took for granted, would ensure the victory of the Entente. My argument that, on the contrary, it would galvanise Austria and rally 7,000,000 reluctant Southern Slavs in her defence, was not listened to, and Grey used the interesting argument that 'ragged fringes' were inevitable at any great territorial settlement. None the less, my prophecy was soon justified to the full, but so far from claiming any credit for it, I am more than ever convinced to-day that no one who knew even the A.B.C. of the question could have reached any other conclusion. In all this we of course had the full and unreserved backing of Masaryk, to whom this incident provided proofs of the alarming ignorance still prevalent in England on all matters connected with the Dual Monarchy, but who naturally enough felt that while losing no opportunity of pleading the Jugoslav cause, he must reserve his main effort for Bohemia and do nothing which could offend official opinion. For this reason also he was very careful to avoid anything which might be construed as anti-Italian, while never wasting an opportunity of smoothing down misunderstandings between his Italian friends and the Jugoslav exiles.

As a result of his conversations with Mr George Clerk Masaryk lost no time in preparing a memorandum suitable for confidential circulation, and at his request I revised the English version for him, found a printer, saw it through the press and myself addressed and posted it to a very carefully selected list of persons. It was called 'Independent Bohemia'. Despite all our care (only 200 were printed and every one was numbered off on my list) it must have found its way through some neutral country to Germany; for it first became generally known by being published in its entirety as an appendix to Karl Friedrich Nowak's 'Chaos' soon after the war. The secretary of a certain neutral Legation in London tried to obtain four copies from the printers, and though I refused to supply them, some other channel was evidently found.

The contents of the Memorandum, which fitted on to my résumé of Masaryk's views at Rotterdam, are well known through the President's own Memoirs; but as they are the first attempt to give clear definition to Czechoslovak aims, they are printed as an appendix on p. 116. Such a document was absolutely necessary, in view of the wide ignorance of public men: but as it was rather long for harassed statesmen, Steed suggested that Masaryk should make an 'abstract' such as Clerk might show to Sir Edward Grey, whose eyesight was already beginning to fail.

V—MASARYK TO SETON-WATSON

26. iv. 15—Monday, 4 p.m. *Kingsley Hotel, London.*

"Dear Mr Seton-Watson,

It is very difficult to be shorter: Mr Steed suggested [that] Sir [Edward] Grey would have an abstract made, should it be too long for him. Mr Clerk could tell you after perusing the Memorandum—type-written or printed—whether I should make the abstract myself. That would detain [me] one or two days longer in London.

The Memorandum is written with the purpose to hand it to

some French, Italian and Russian friends. Would you approve of doing that? I hope you will find the time to correct the Memorandum. I thank you very much for doing so and for every suggestion you would make me."

* * *

Meanwhile the idea of a Hus celebration on the 500th anniversary of his death had already been taken up in several quarters, and while Geneva was very rightly selected for the major demonstration—where Masaryk and Ernest Denis delivered addresses in the Salle de la Réformation on 6 July—we were eager to organise something similar in England, though necessarily on a smaller scale. Masaryk went down to Oxford, where we stayed with Sir Arthur Evans on Boar's Hill, and after a couple of days' lobbying we succeeded in obtaining the signatures of twenty or thirty of the leading men in the University, in all branches of learning, for a letter on Hus and Bohemia which appeared in *The Times* of 6 July. On the same day a most successful meeting was held at the Aeolian Hall, with Lord Bryce in the chair. Unfortunately we came out into a thunderstorm and really torrential rain and during the crowd and confusion our chairman was relieved of a presentation gold watch and chain, which the Czech Colony gallantly subscribed to replace. Two days earlier I had given a special Hus lecture at King's College, London, with Dean Wace in the chair.

Masaryk was of course by this time back in Switzerland, having stopped on the way through Paris to plan the publication of *La Nation Tchèque*, under the editorship of his friend Ernest Denis. But before he left, he had given his full backing to the Jugoslav Committee, whose leading members under Dr Trumbić arrived in London and published their 'Manifesto to the British Nation'. Once again I was plunged into the work of editing, translating, printing and distributing: but in this case my main task was to screw them up to more rapid action than they had supposed to be necessary. Three days running Steed and I sent them urgent telegrams, warning them that they would 'miss the bus', and that we should wash our hands of them if they came too late. It was a real race against time, for it was necessary to peg out as publicly as possible the Jugoslav claim to Dalmatia before Italy entered the war, and therefore before the censorship imposed possible restrictions upon criticism of our new ally. In the end the manifesto duly appeared, a week before the actual entry of Italy, and obtained a new and sympathetic publicity.

I pass over the letters which I received from Masaryk during May, except for a single quotation. 'In the first letter (I use card to facilitate the censor's work), I wish to express to you my feeling of gratitude: I appreciate all you have done for me and my work.' At that moment he intended visiting Rome, 'to meet an influential man from Petrograd', and asked Steed for introductions to Sonnino, Salandra and Sir Rennell Rodd. He was happy to announce the arrival of the Agrarian deputy Dürich from Prague, and wrote: 'He is willing to go with me *jusqu'au bout* and I am glad of course not to be alone any more.' But he soon was disillusioned, for Dürich proved himself to be the tool of extreme Russian reactionaries, and the resulting scandal caused regrettable dissensions among the Czechs abroad.

The journey to Rome had to be abandoned not merely because of the Dürich affair, but also because of grave news from Prague.

VI—Masaryk to Seton-Watson

Geneva. *9. 6. 15.*

"My dear Mr Seton-Watson,

Dr Kramář and Dr Scheiner were arrested at the command of the Generalissimo Archduke Friedrich; they were brought to Vienna: there they are tried, Kramář for having given information to the Russians, Scheiner for having committed *crimen laesae majestatis*. I hear the imprisonment of both leaders has stirred our political public: I wish it would. In Prague people live too much perhaps under the impression of the Russian strategy: but this is easily to be understood.

I wrote you that I might go to Rome to see there a Russian official man: he went to Albania, and it seems he has difficulties to come back from Valona. The Italians did not like that he went, and tried to prevent it: it shows the Russians control what the Italians do there, though of course he went to control the Austrians.

More and more I think of going to Petrograd.

I hear our friend of Rjeka is going back to Petrograd: I think it is not the right moment to speak there much of Dalmatia, etc. I have some information which makes me think so. These informations are of a personal character: they do not like our friend. They received him first as coming from London, but later they disliked him.

And then, they do not like the Serbian Minister [Dr Spalajković]. I fear they would not like to hear the Jugoslav wishes expressed by the[se] two politicians. Besides they are nervous now....

Yours truly, T. G. MASARYK."

VII—MASARYK TO SETON-WATSON

Geneva, 23. vi. 1915 (not censored). (*Hôtel de la Poste.*)

"You will find among the different incoherent news some valuable hints for our friends: please show them to Mr Steed and have them forwarded to the competent authority. In Bern, I fear, the British Embassy was not prepared to get these news and to send them (I asked that in London). I will continue to send these news to you, until another way will be assured....

Our Fiume friend was here: he left for Paris. I suppose you soon will see him. He is very much depressed by what he experienced in Petrograd.

About the Russian retreat. I would now say only this: *it is possible* that this retreat is caused not only by the alleged want of ammunition, but also by the WANT OF RIFLES. It is curious that the Russian *reserve* is not called to join the army—what does that mean? Of course my explanation is only a hypothesis: I call your and our friends' attention to it, because I fear that the Russians would be ashamed to tell the true reason of their retreat and defeat, and there is no time any more for such 'diplomacy'. The Allies must be clear about the real position of each member, and face things in earnest. Goodbye.

Yours, R. ALG. MILL."

* * *

The references in these two letters are to Frano Supilo, whom Masaryk rightly regarded as head and shoulders above all the other Yugoslav exiles, not excluding Trumbić himself. Supilo was a self-made man, editor of a small Croat paper called *Novi List*, which he published in Fiume because the censorship was less stringent in that autonomous city than in either Croatia or Dalmatia. Unfortunately Supilo could not suffer fools gladly. He fell foul of Mr Bošković, the Serbian Minister in London, a completely incompetent diplomat, whose narrow Pan-Serb outlook led him to refuse to introduce the Jugoslav Committee to the Foreign Office, unless certain passages relating to Jugoslav Unity were deleted. He also fell foul of certain leading Russian statesmen, whose abysmal ignorance of the Southern Slav question came as a profound disillusionment. This indifference to the fate of the Dalmatian Croats so long as the tiny Orthodox Serb minority could be saved, seemed to him nothing short of treason. Moreover, he was appalled at some of the things which he learned in Petrograd about the state of the Russian army, and he was the first to bring back to London the full facts about the traitor Colonel Myasoyedov, and his share in the disaster of Tannenberg.

These letters illustrate the realism with which Masaryk faced the disappointments and dangers of the first year of war: and it is worth noting that this letter alone of the seventy in my possession was signed with a pseudonym.

While Masaryk was at Geneva our little group of Czechophils in London had the idea that the best means of introducing him to the British public would be to find him a post at one of the British Universities, where his unique qualities as a scholar and a teacher could not fail to impress academic circles. The following letter of 25 June 1915 explains itself.

VIII—SETON-WATSON TO T. G. MASARYK

"I think I told you of my scheme for the foundation of a School of Slavonic Studies at London University—for Russian, but *also* for Polish, Czech and South Slav. The Principal of King's College, Dr Burrows (a keen Philhellene and also a member of the Serbian Relief Fund Committee and a friend of the Serbs) took up the idea eagerly. A room has been assigned for the formation of a Slavonic library later on, and it is hoped to found a Chair at the University, with the help of the Government.

The next stage was to arrange for next winter a course of preliminary lectures on Slav History and Literature in the widest sense ('Slav Tendencies' or 'The Slavonic Idea' I should prefer to call them) and I definitely suggested to Burrows that *you* should be invited to be the first lecturer—for next winter only, of course, as we hope and indeed *know* that you will have other and more important work to do later on. This would give a great impetus to the whole idea and arouse interest and attention, as well as giving you and the Bohemian cause a special entrée in London.

I have now got Burrows's answer. He officially asks me to approach you in the matter and to invite you to consider seriously your acceptance of the post of lecturer on Slavonic History and Literature (or a similar title to be arranged later), from October next until Christmas. The appointment would be for a year, but if you found it impossible to lecture *after* Christmas the winter course would be sufficient. There would not be more than two lectures a week, and you would be given absolute and complete latitude as to treatment of the subject. The idea is to treat the Slavs as a whole, from the 'literary and historico-philosophical' side. The University would see that you had a representative audience—not *merely* students. We should get special chairmen to introduce you, and the course would be published afterwards, and we should try to give as much publicity as possible.

May I urge you *very strongly* on my own behalf to accept? I am sure it is much the most practical way of arousing interest for the cause you have most at heart. So far as the pecuniary side is concerned, there would of course be a salary attached to the appointment...."

* * *

After an interval of ten days there came the following characteristic answer. He needed some persuasion, and indeed in his Memoirs he has recorded that at the time he looked upon the University post as 'a bothersome interruption—though to-day I understand that Seton-Watson and Burrows advised me well when they urged me so insistently to accept the appointment'.*

IX—Masaryk to Seton-Watson

Geneva. 8. vii. 1915.

"...Your plan is excellent, I told you in London: but I am not quite sure that I would be the lecturer you wish and expect. Allow me to give my reasons for this scepticism.

I. I begin with the statement that I will be in London without my library. I have in Prague a pretty good collection of Slav books, etc.: in London I will have nothing, and I do not see how I could work without the aid of my books and studies.

Of course there are books in the British Museum and elsewhere, but I doubt whether the collection is sufficient. Besides, I would lose a great deal of time, being obliged to work out of doors.

Such a course as you propose, I should think, requires a library accessible to the students: they must see some books, maps, etc., else the lecture would be too abstract. And I expect that the interest for the Slav nations would lead the students to get the

* *The Making of a State*, p. 100.

necessary knowledge of the sources for their studies. Is it possible to provide such a library? Since the war, it is impossible for me to get Russian, Polish and even Bohemian books: for instance, the whole Russian war literature is not accessible. (By the way: I ordered some books from Petrograd: if you will allow me, I will write to the bookseller to send them for me to you.)

II. The students will perhaps wish to be informed of the Slav languages, therefore of the different grammars, dictionaries, etc. Many students will wish to be acquainted with the history, with the literature. I would not be able to come up to those expectations without a good library, because I am a layman in this department.

III. The Slavic studies were subordinate in my scientific career: as you see from my first book (on Suicide), it is Sociology and Ethics (with Philosophy of Religion) which interested me directly. Then I became a politician: although I tried to be well informed in all Slavic questions I would not dare to call me [myself] a Slavist. I know Bohemia and Russia tolerably well, the rest only a little. I doubt therefore whether I have the right to lecture even on such a theme as you propose. Yet I think I could give a tolerably good lecture on Sociological Introduction to the Study of the Slav Nations—or something of this kind, but only in case I would be able to get my books, which I will try very seriously. (In fact, I tried, but in vain.)

IV. But there is one great drawback to the plan—my political work. I know I often will have to go to Paris (from London), perhaps I will be required in Geneva, even in Rome, Nish or Petrograd. I suppose I am not allowed to take the position at the University, not feeling quite free for the work. And just this work requires regularity and real science: it would be a pity to frighten people [away from?] the Slav. Studies.

I therefore conclude that to be quite honest I do not dare to say Yes, as long as I do not know what my political and scientific (library, etc.) circumstances will be in October and later on. Mr Burrows may try to find another lecturer: should he not succeed, perhaps he can decide in October. At that time—even sooner, in September—I hope to be able to say a decided Yes or No.

I agree with you that this position would provide a special entrée in London, and I would be really happy if I could serve your plan: but I hope you will understand my hesitation. At any rate please explain the reasons given to Mr Burrows. Meanwhile I try to gather as many Slavic books as possible.

I expect a member of the Prague Chamber of Commerce, and then we will come out into the open. Terrorism in Prague is very strong now: they watch the communication with us, and I'm sorry to tell that they succeed in finding out the persons concerned. Some days ago the deputy Rašín, a friend of Dr Kramář, was imprisoned, and I think because of his connection with Geneva.

He was a great help to me. How they found out that he is our help, that requires a longer explanation. I will give it in London: it is very interesting....

On the 6th we had a very good meeting. Denis gave an impressive lecture: we had 1200 hearers, in fact [the] whole [of] Geneva. All papers brought articles, it is a great success...."

* * *

It was not until late in September 1915 that Masaryk was free to return to London. The two months following the Hus celebrations had been fully occupied planning the activities of the National Committee and gathering a small group of absolutely devoted followers round him. At the beginning of September the man who was to become his official collaborator and heir of his ideas, Edward Beneš, escaped into Switzerland, and it was arranged between them that while Beneš should act as secretary in the Paris office, Masaryk himself should live in London, and devote himself to making the Czech cause known in England and to maintaining and extending the all-important contacts with America. The third of the triumvirate to which Czechoslovakia owed its creation was the young Slovak astronomer and airman,

Milan Štefaník, who used to full advantage his many contacts in French society, and first introduced Beneš to some of the leading French politicians. The alliance of these three men was an ideal one, and far outweighed such feather-weights as Dürich. It was entirely untrammelled by conventions, but it rested on a sense of reality and very great tactical skill. They were always in the right place at the right moment.

Two little incidents of this period, very trifling in themselves, acquire a certain piquancy in the light of the present situation. On 18 July the Polish Committee in London organised a concert of Polish and Czech music which was intended as a demonstration in favour of a common struggle for independence. Later in the month a special reception in honour of Bohemia, attended by many prominent members of the political world and addressed by Lord Bryce and other speakers, was held at the house of Mrs Runciman, who twenty-three years later was to accompany her husband on a famous but melancholy mission to Prague.

Once settled in London, Masaryk allowed himself to be persuaded that the professor in him must keep his place beside the politician. On 19 October he gave at King's College the inaugural lecture of our new School of Slavonic Studies. Burrows, not without the sympathetic help of the Foreign Office, had succeeded in securing no less a chairman than the Prime Minister himself, and our disappointment was therefore keen when Mr Asquith was prevented by illness from attending. Happily, however, his place was worthily filled by Lord Robert Cecil, then Under-Secretary for Foreign Affairs: and so began an association which was to last for more than two decades, and in which the names of Cecil and Beneš were to be identified with the cause of the new Genevan World Order. The subject of the lecture was 'The Problem of Small Nations in the European Crisis', and in it Masaryk pointed out that there was a huge more or less triangular zone lying between Germany and Russia, or between the Baltic, the Adriatic, the Aegean and the Black Sea, which was 'the real and proper centre of national antagonism'. This 'danger zone' was in itself 'the most urgent and clamant cause for remodelling the political organisation of Europe'. Most of the nationalities inhabiting it had once been free and were now striving for independence. And as against them Germany, possessed by pan-Germanic theory, was pursuing the aim of World-Power for the Herrenvolk. 'We can and must accept political realism,' declared this truly Realist philosopher, 'but we never can approve of the Realpolitik of Treitschke, Mommsen, Lagarde, Bernhardi and others who have converted anthropology into zoology. I say that, though I am speaking in the country of Darwin and his theory of the survival of the so-called fittest.' His plea for the small nations as true exponents of culture naturally drew some of its illustrations from the history of the Czechs and Serbs, and he confessed at the close to a certain scepticism. 'Is this a time for talking about small nations, when the vital thing is simply to afford protection to one of them? Feeling this incongruity, I will comfort myself with the saying of a Slav thinker, "A good word is a deed also".'

The moment selected for the lecture was an anxious one for all Slavs, for Serbia was on the point of being overrun by the Central Powers, and Masaryk, like many of his British friends, felt keenly the procrastination and false tactics which rendered possible the great tragedy of the Serb retreat across Albania. He felt also, but was too proud and too tactful to express openly, a certain disappointment that the message of apology sent by Mr Asquith, while paying tribute to his own personal qualities, and reaffirming the resolve of the Allies to defend the liberties of small nations, should have linked his name with Russia and with Serbia, without even mentioning Bohemia. It is worth adding that ten years later, in 1925, in the same hall, Mr Asquith (now Lord Oxford and Asquith) took the chair at an anniversary lecture of our School delivered by Dr Beneš, as Foreign Minister of an independent Czechoslovak state.

The following letter explains itself. Masaryk had crossed the Channel on a Serbian passport, by special arrangement with the

Foreign Office. One morning he telephoned to tell me that the police were suspicious of him and would not let him leave the house. I spent a hectic day getting the necessary messages to two of the busiest men in London, Mr Clerk at the Foreign Office and Sir Edward Henry, Commissioner of Police: but by nightfall the over-zealous inspector had received reassuring messages from the authorities, and Masaryk, who was henceforth unmolested, fully recognised that under war conditions the local police were perfectly justified in their attitude. Something of the same sort used to happen to Dr Beneš every time he crossed the Channel, and Steed in his memoirs gives a humorous account of his warning the British Passport officer at Havre that before very long 'this Beenees' might be signing passports himself, as the Minister of a free country.*

X—MASARYK TO SETON-WATSON

4 Holford Road, Hampstead, 27. xi. 1915.

"My dear Mr Seton-Watson,

The history of the policeman (Detective Mr Miles—Criminal Investigation Dept., Police Station, Rosslyn Hill, Hampstead) has a rather unpleasant continuation. He came to-day to investigate my passport, which he copied yesterday: I suppose he informed himself meanwhile, that Moravia (where I am born) is not in Serbia, and he wished to know how I could have got a Serbian passport. He asked, I answered the questions. Then he advised me to go to the Police Station Albany Street (tube Camden Town) and ask there to be registered.

I went. The officer decided to acknowledge the Serbian passport, and that there is no need of registration. That is my opinion also and therefore I did not go to the police when I came here. They can enquire at the Serbian Embassy in Paris whether I have got the passport in an orderly way, for they can doubt that, etc.:

* *Through Thirty Years*, p. 100.

but they were bound to acknowledge the Serbian passport, if they do not believe that it is falsified.

I beg you to insist on this, for only a passport gives me the possibility to travel, etc.

MASARYK."

* * *

The Serbian tragedy caused Masaryk much anxious thinking, and as the second winter of the war dragged on and his means of judging the facts of the situation increased, he became increasingly critical of the policy of the Allies, their conduct of the war, and above all the lack of unity in military operations. Here is a letter prompted by this mood.

XI—MASARYK TO SETON-WATSON

30. xi. 1915.

"My dear Mr Seton-Watson,

Many thanks for your interventions!

Your remark on the Staff prompts me to some further remarks. The Bagdad affair: one would expect that the Staff and the War Office and Grey would wish to counterbalance the Balkan defeat by the capture of Bagdad—they advance, but the next day they announce that they had no — water (!) and to-day we read: the Turks have too large forces to be driven out! It is incredible: they did not know that they will want water, and they did not know what forces the enemy disposes of.

And the Kitchener meandering: the supreme war-lord engaged in diplomatic work, and the supposition that he must *see* the situation in the Near East!

I can imagine how the Germans laugh. Or take that instance yesterday: *The Times* correspondent (a Colonel) demonstrates that the Germans cannot reach Constantinople, etc.—the very same day the German Headquarters shows that the junction will be perfect in a short time, they only have to restore the rails.

And what superstitious talking one could read about the impenetrable Serbian mountains! By the way, the London papers are execrable, wretchedly bad, all of them. Even the war correspondents. E.g. the correspondent of *The Times* brings one day figures showing the amount of the Russian forces: the next day he continues, brings new figures: if you take your pencil and verify the two data, you find out that either the first or the second is wrong (perhaps both).

I once told you that the *Round Table* men should have a critical weekly: I think that something of the kind is absolutely necessary to lead the public opinion and above all to lead the Government and the Staff. The *New Statesman* is one of the better weeklies, but not sufficient at all: it has a more narrow aim and is narrow in its political aspirations. What I would wish would be the embodiment of the English conscience and political and strategic thinking.

Allow me finally one word about the Police affair. I appreciate the fact that they researched matters as soon as their attention was directed to me: that was their duty. But the way they did it revealed to my observation an abyss of the most unthinking bureaucratism. If I take it as a symptom and a part of the administration, the judgment could not be favourable, and it confirms the general observation and experience.

Yours, T. G. MASARYK."

* * *

As a result of much thought and discussion on these things, he wrote at our request a Memorandum entitled 'At the Eleventh Hour', devoted especially to a criticism of the military situation. It has never been published in any language, and I therefore make no apology for printing it now. It will be found in Chapter v. There were doubtless certain errors of judgment and perspective in the Memorandum, but nothing is more characteristic of his keen critical sense, his power of vision, and perhaps above all his fearlessness, nay his audacity, in launching such an indictment in a country to which he had come as a little-known exile, and in which he was still feeling his way. On the other hand, to those who had ears to hear, this increased the effect twofold, for in every phrase there was transparent honesty and a burning desire to win the war, and he stood forth as one who had staked everything he had, and the very future of his race, on an Allied victory.

XII—Autograph Notes of T. G. M.

[The following rough notes, undated, but belonging to the early winter of 1915, have been selected somewhat at random from a much larger *dossier*, as an indication of the sort of material which Masaryk used to obtain from his secret channels, and which I of course handed on to the proper authorities. By Christmas direct contact had been established, and loss of time in communication had been reduced to a minimum.]

"A. *Italy*. (Source, a very influential man coming from Rome.) Italy says she is driven to Germany because the Entente has no plan.

B. *Polish Workmen in Germany*. (Source, Budget Commission of Reichstag.)

300,000 working men from Russian Poland replaced that number of German workmen sent to the Army.

Berlin-Bagdad. (The same source.)

In the circle of Delbrück, Bethmann Hollweg, etc., the peace question was discussed: it was urged that Germany must come to an understanding with England. For England, in fact, was not beaten: on the contrary, she has the supremacy on the sea and has got the German Colonies. First an attempt will be made to threaten Britain by a fierce attack on Calais: if it should fail, Germany would be willing to make peace. Germany could concede that she has been beaten on the sea and that England must have the supremacy of commerce, they themselves being satisfied to be the first producer. If necessary, the Germans would cede Heligoland, to enable the English to control the Kiel Canal: they would even allow the English to have a direct control of that canal during fifty years. The Germans give up the sea, being content to have Central Europe. Of course their merchant fleet would grow meanwhile. The territory of France, Belgium, Poland, will be cleared: only some regulation of the Russian frontier might be necessary.

The plan means to separate England from the Allies, to strengthen anti-Russian suspicions, to play the comedy of maritime inferiority, but prepare the final attack on England from Constantinople. Central Europe is much more worth than contested supremacy at sea, which of course will be given by itself if Germany should control the Adriatic and the Aegean. I think there is some danger in that plan: people who did not realise what Berlin-Bagdad means will be pleased to have the supremacy of the sea.

I am not quite sure whether the plan has been shaped as it was given, but I think I can see so much: that the Germans will try to cheat English diplomacy, turning attention from the Continent and pushing the English on to the sea—in other words, the Germans will try to strengthen the fault of English policy consisting in the neglect of the Continent and pursuing a one-sided so-called sea-policy.

C. *Confidential information received by Masaryk via Amsterdam* (sent off 12 December, but only received 18).

(1) Dr Goričar who, as you will probably know from the English and American papers up to this time, started that great campaign against the German-Austrian espionage, is now no more a solitary case. This circumstance, so far as I know, is kept in the dark by the Government in Vienna.

This concerns specially the late Austrian consul in Port Said, von Probinger, who was transferred in December last year to Salonica. Last summer he got sick leave, which he went to spend in Switzerland, but from there he went to Italy, handed in his papers for dismissal and now got the Italian naturalisation certificate. The rage against him at the Foreign Office in Vienna is inexpressible: and it should be remarked that further surprises of this kind are not impossible.

Dr Goričar's deserts in the cause of international justice, his manly step to check the band of conspirators in the United States, are far greater than the public can imagine. Otherwise one can see already the fruits of his efforts, and that is the pleasantest thing of all.

(2) The action against Dr Kramář, Dr Rašín and editor Cervinka began on 6th instant before the court-martial in Vienna. At the same time this tribunal requested the Public Prosecutor in Prague to collect an open report as to the amount of all the property of the defendants, in whatever form, and falling under the autonomy of the Austrian authorities.

According to the report of the *Prager Zeitung* of 8th or 9th instant, the tribunal at Prague—in its capacity as a criminal court, naturally—let the requested investigation take place, and sanctioned the confiscation of the amount, 'in reparation for all and any of the incommodities which the criminal actions of the accused may have brought to the state'. This is the plainest example of mediaeval justice one can imagine.

According to the official accusation Dr Kramář is prosecuted for high treason and espionage, the other two are accused of espionage. It is given out that the prosecution will take several weeks. My personal opinion is that this could hardly be the case, as the Austrian Court-Martial is very well known as 'expeditive'. Neither have I the least doubt that the utmost possible penalty will be proposed (viz. the penalty of death), so that probably afterwards the comedy of the appeal for reducing the sentence may be performed.

(3) Your daughter, Miss Alice, was brought with the other fellow-prisoners (Dušek, Kuntz, etc.) to Vienna, where, however, as I have been assured, the treatment is such as to leave nothing better to be wished for.

(4) Your wife is getting on well enough as regards her personal health, according to a report of 28 November 1915.

(5) In *our* circles at Prague it is to be mentioned that the new Chief of the Police, Dr Kuntz, discovered Pangermanistic

machinations—among the German-Bohemian deputies—which led to the imprisonment of Dr Urban. I report this with all reserve, as I have not yet got any confirmation of the matter, but I will, however, not forget to come to this matter again later on.

(6) About three weeks ago Hermann Bahr* stayed again in Prague, in order to collect information as to the disposition in Prague. The greatest impression was made upon him, it is reported, by the interview with old Dr Mattuš who, with the authority of age and experience, gave him to understand that we Czechs cannot attain to anything as decided anti-Austrians and anti-Germans.

Dr Mattuš† really is—by all his personal conduct during the war—perhaps the only politician in Bohemia who deserves the name.

(7) On the other side what Dr Fiedler‡ is doing, for instance, who is all aflame for the 'close connection' with Austria, is directly against political foresight and against elementary national decency. On his side worthily stand 'Národní Listy', which under the absolute leadership of Dr Tobolka, together with 'Pravo Lidu', emulate one another in subservience and boot-licking. I mention these pathological circumstances only because they, to the great pleasure of every patriot, stand quite solitary, and the steely determination and unanimity of almost all our people is thus put into the right light.

There were some rumours a short time ago, when the Cabinet in Vienna was reconstructed, that Fiedler and Viškovsky are to be appointed Ministers. It was not very likely: all the same—thank God—it was not confirmed.

* The well-known Austrian dramatist and novelist, who also wrote *Austriaca* and *Dalmatinische Reise*, with sympathetic references to Masaryk.

† A Czech Elder Statesman long ere this in retirement, who originally belonged to the bodyguard of the Old Czech leader Dr Rieger, and was latterly a member of the Austrian Herrenhaus.

‡ A Czech ex-Minister, with whom Masaryk was in political collaboration.

(8) As to the state of public opinion, the best proof is the festival performance of 'Hlubička' ['The Kiss', by Smetana], 12 October, which *had* to be given as a part of the celebration for Archduke Franz Salvator.

After the introductory Austrian hymn a hardly audible applause was heard, and the overture to the opera was accepted with demonstrative approval.

This performance, as well as the visit of Franz Salvator to Prague, forms really only one link of a chain of visits of the dynasty to Prague.

Soon after this the successor to the throne, as well as the Archduke, came to Prague to win public opinion for Vienna: that this should be a lost endeavour still seems to these people incomprehensible.

(9) The relations between Austria and Germany—especially as regards military circles—do not seem to be rosy. It is said that General Tersztyanszky, in a controversy with Mackensen owing to German influence, had to resign, and was decorated with one of the highest orders.

The resignation of MM. Schuster, Herold and Engel proves that satisfactory economic relations between Austria and Germany are not without danger.

(10) The introduction of the new Ministers Hohenlohe, Spitzmüller and...?...is interpreted to mean that in the action for mutual understanding no concessions were made to Hungary, and if possible—for the fourth war loan which is to be expected in March—that the Parliament is to be summoned (on Körber's proposition). One can understand that they, as a consequence of the great economic catastrophe which has now broken out in the whole of Austria-Hungary, would like to shift the responsibility from the 'men of foresight' on to the 'people'!

(11) I don't know whether you follow the course of the Austrian crown. Nothing can give a more perfect impression of the economic catastrophe than that. The last Dutch course (15 December) gives 30.70 guilders for 100 Kr. instead of the

usual course of about 50. In Vienna the price of 100 guilders is 310 Kr. (instead of the usual 199). The fall in the course of German Marks during the last few days on all the Exchanges (here, even to 44.30!!) is an infallible sign of the economic agony.

(12) According to the reports circulated in Vienna there seems to be a spy among the people who come into closest contact with the German Emperor. I mention this only as a curiosity.

Furthermore, I have learned from a very reliable source, that whole districts in Alsace-Lorraine were undermined, and the French are to be drawn into the ambush.

One follows the reports of the Balkan expedition with great tension here [Amsterdam] and everybody wishes, unanimously, that England would know how to look at the immense significance of this theatre of the war."

XIII—Masaryk to Seton-Watson

[Enclosing notes which have not been preserved].

10. 1. 1916.

"My dear Seton-Watson, please forward these informations: as Dr Beneš was detained in Holland more than a week, the informations were delayed. Next time we must find a way to stop these delays.

They are given by an Austrian official residing in Germany: the *facts* are exact, his deductions are of course of a personal character.

Yours, Masaryk."

* * *

Towards the end of January Masaryk was called over to Paris, and there are a number of letters relating to political matters which required attention during his absence—among others the unrealised idea of publishing his lectures at the University.

XIV—MASARYK TO SETON-WATSON

Palais d'Orsay, 7. ii. 1916.

"My dear Mr Seton-Watson,

I find here what I expected to find—a quick grasping of the situation, if it is reasonably explained. All the leading papers bring articles on the significance of an independent Bohemia, and are writing more and more against Austria.

I hear a good deal of important news. The Italians are strongly opposed to our Bohemian plans—they are pro-Magyar and very much anti-Serb: I am told that I must go to Rome. Perhaps it would be advisable that you should go too? M. Briand is going there, and I suppose he will touch the Bohemian and other questions.

I cannot send all news, as long as I am not sure that you get them: therefore I am sending only few, and of minor importance.

I am adapting the Memorandum to the situation here, and besides I wrote an abstract for my friends here.

Yours sincerely, MASARYK."

* * *

The Memorandum to which this letter refers was the fruit of Masaryk's growing alarm and impatience at the progress of the war, or rather at the lack of progress and indeed the steady deterioration of Allied plans, in so far as they could be said to exist at all. It was based upon close personal observation of British public opinion as expressed in the Press, in current literature (of both of which he was a voracious reader), and in the cinema; and above all upon constant conversations with men in every rank and condition of life. His inner circle of friends, who were also gravely disquieted by the march of events, encouraged him in the idea of committing his unvarnished views to paper. As before, I undertook the Englishing of his manuscript, its passage through the press and its distribution to a list of persons doubly and trebly checked and tested as likely not merely not to take offence, but to accept it, not necessarily as accurate in every fact and opinion put forward, but as a real contribution to the war effort, from one who had staked everything upon Allied victory.

It certainly was not without its effect, if only because it made his name and objects familiar to many of those who 'counted' most. In the perspective of a quarter of a century it seems to me to rank as one of the most trenchant and realistic political criticisms during the whole period of the Great War.

The full text of the Memorandum, which has not hitherto been published, will be found in Chapter v.

Such being his considered views upon the conduct of the war, it was only logical that he should feel the desperate need for an organ of opinion capable of guiding a public opinion which in the sphere of foreign politics was still very largely a sheep without a shepherd. It was in this mood that he wrote the two following letters.

XV—MASARYK TO SETON-WATSON

Tollard Royal Hotel, Bournemouth, 2. v. 1916.

"My dear Seton-Watson,

I think you must start 'The Weekly' at once, without delay: all other plans (going to Russia, to Rome, etc.) are now of no importance at all. You cannot depend on the collaboration of Russians and French: yourself (British) must be able and determined to criticise your Government, etc., and you must be able to say what must be done.

I imagine you will convoke your friends (and by their help some other people), appoint the staff of editors and have the first number printed and published in 2 weeks (latest). There is no minute any more for waiting.

If you analyse what Kut, Ireland, the recruiting failure mean, you must come to the conclusion that the Government and the General Staff (*and the Navy*) have no plan at all. ...., one sees, is incapable of leading also. Therefore I don't see any other plan than to gather a group of thinking men and speak publicly: the Press is unable, they only criticise *ex post facto*, negatively.

S.-W., Burrows, Evans, Baird, Steed, Gooch, Hyndman, Holland Rose, etc.*

Mr Stumpf will bring you my sketch of the Weekly."

(Enclosure.)

Suggestions for NUMBER ONE *of the new paper*

"Some introductory remarks (not long—no promises, a simple statement of the need of the weekly!).

Kut. (What the surrender of the Kut Army means: all the defects and shortcomings of policy, military organisation, strategy, etc. This analysis gives an appalling picture and a pretty full register of the so-called 'muddle').

Is criticism easy? (A refutation of all the stupidity one hears in Parliament against criticism, etc.)

What Germany has accomplished. (The partial realisation of the Pan-German plan.)

Austria-Hungary, the tool of Prussian militarism.

What plan has Great Britain with Turkey?

Weekly review of facts.

Weekly review of papers, etc., etc."

* These were, the present writer: Dr Ronald Burrows, Principal of King's College and a leading Philhellene and close friend of Venizelos: Sir Arthur Evans, the Cretan explorer and the doyen of South Slav studies in this country: Major John Baird, afterwards Lord Stonehaven, at that time in the War Office Intelligence: H. W. Steed, foreign editor, and afterwards editor, of *The Times*: G. P. Gooch, the historian: H. M. Hyndman, the veteran exponent of Marxism in this country, whose wife, Rosalind Hyndman, was keenly interested in Finland and the subject nationalities of Austria-Hungary: Holland Rose, the biographer of Napoleon and William Pitt.

XVI—MASARYK TO SETON-WATSON

Bournemouth, 3. v. 1916.

"My dear Seton-Watson,

The need of the Weekly can be proved by comparing similar papers or magazines. Take for instance the *New Statesman*, the last number. The criticism of Naumann's book (*Mitteleuropa*) gives a wrong impression of the book and its aims. Because it speaks calmly, not roughly, the critic almost accepts it, not finding any cynicism in Naumann, etc. In fact this calmness is the fullest cynicism, hiding by smooth words the most brutal tendency. In the same number you find a long criticism of a book depicting Shakespeare as a staunch Germanophobe: no doubt that is childish, but the *New Statesman* is unjust and one-sided, because he does not show that the Germans do the same. And he devotes a *long* article to his task—by that the reader is misled, he loses the right proportion of things, he is educated in a Germanophil spirit. Take farther in consideration that the *New Statesman* protects the Government, and you will understand if I say that this paper does not teach to think, and that it is positively wrong and harmful. I read the *Statesman* since a year almost, and cannot approve of it at all: and this week it pretends to be a *New* political guide! Just the whole tendency, the spirit of 'The Weekly', I hope would be different, and truly *new*: it must teach people to think and to imagine, and it must be new; it must be the organ of *literary revolution*, if a political revolution is impossible.

Of course you must expect that the Government will be against *The Weekly*: you must be prepared to issue and to circulate *The Weekly* against official suppressive measures.

I did not say it, but it is a matter of course that I would work for you: my going to Rome or Petrograd has almost no sense if Great Britain should fail, and she will fail if an open, strong and able *protesting* movement will not be organised.

I enclose the contents of the first number.

Yours, MASARYK."

* * *

In a third letter he brought forward other arguments to prove the 'absolute necessity' of such a weekly—for instance, the tremendous delays which had occurred before the value of Emanuel Voska as a worker in the Allied cause in America came to be recognised by the British authorities, and again the case of a Czech naval engineer—a proved expert in highly confidential inventive work—who had been interned early in the war and who, despite repeated representations, was not released for nearly two years, long after the War Office had recognised that 'this man must not remain idle'.

My own contribution to this period of 'Sturm und Drang' had been, apart from a series of books and pamphlets, an article entitled 'The Failure of Sir Edward Grey' in the *English Review*.* My punishment for this frankness of speech was an official veto upon my employment in an Allied country. Our Ambassador in Petrograd, Sir George Buchanan, had asked that I should be sent out as a kind of liaison with the Balkan and Austrian Slavs in Russia, working with Bernard Pares and Harold Williams, the two foremost British authorities of the day on Russian politics: and it had been decided that I should accompany Sir Samuel Hoare, who had just been appointed liaison officer between the War Office and the Russian military authorities. My passport and tickets were all ready, and I had already said goodbye to my family, when a telegram came, finally cancelling the whole plan. From my own selfish point of view I have always regretted, not that I had made myself officially unacceptable by publishing criticism which I then believed to be vital to the country's interests and which events have in the main justified, but because I was thus deprived of the supreme adventure of my life, the chance of living through the final stages of the Russian Revolution. Masaryk, though much annoyed at the mentality which prompted this decision, made an immediate and concentrated onslaught upon me, and did not rest until he had persuaded our little group to risk the publication of a weekly review entitled *The New Europe*.

* Reprinted in *Europe in the Melting Pot* (1919), to the Czech edition of which President Masaryk contributed a short preface.

'I think the weekly is an absolute necessity', he wrote on 22 August, 'the more so since the time approaches when the Government must shape a political programme.... I am considering the possibility of publishing a French weekly in Paris, and I would publish an English weekly here, should your weekly not be started. But I hope it will.'

The first number appeared on 17 October, and its first article was a detailed *exposé* of the Pan-German programme by Masaryk himself—illustrated by a coloured sketchmap of the 'Drang nach Osten' (Berlin-Bagdad), which was soon in demand in various quarters and was reprinted separately. The main point of our programme was 'La Victoire Intégrale'. We were to 'provide a rallying-ground for all those who see in European reconstruction, on a basis of nationality, the rights of minorities, and the hard facts of geography and economics, the sole guarantee against an early repetition of the horrors of the present war'. 'After our armies have won the war, our statesmen will have to win the peace, and their task will indeed be difficult unless public opinion is alert, organised and eager to support them in a clearly defined and enlightened policy.' Finally, 'an integral victory, such as alone can secure to Europe permanent peace and the reduction of armaments, the fulfilment of the solemn pledges assumed by our statesmen towards our smaller allies, the vindication of national rights and public law, the emancipation of the subject races of central and south-east Europe from German and Magyar control—such must be our answer to the Pan-German project of "Central Europe" and "Berlin-Bagdad"'.

During the next six months Masaryk contributed a series of five articles on 'The Literature of Pangermanism' and others on 'Austria under Francis Joseph' (on the occasion of his death in November 1916), 'Pangermanism and the Zone of Small Nations', 'Bohemia and the European Crisis' (No. 15), 'The Future Status of Bohemia' (No. 19). 'Russia: from Theocracy to Democracy' contains his first reactions to the first Russian Revolution. One brief extract awakens an echo in the present situation.

'Prussianised Germany united with Russia could divide the world to her heart's content....To-day the great political problem which centres round Great Britain, Russia and Germany overshadows all others: will Great Britain join forces with Russia, or does she consider Germany to be less dangerous to her world-empire than Russia? This is the question which Great Britain has to decide, and on her decision will depend the future of the Old and the New World.' To this may be added an extract from his letter of 16 March 1917: 'Russia has her Tsarism: but she is a living country, much more so than the radical Westerners can conceive. The relatively bloodless revolution shows that great political and social changes begin to be possible, as soon as men are not afraid to risk their lives. The effect on Europe and on the War will be great if the Duma succeeds in establishing the new order and the new Tsar.'

Not the least interesting were his philosophical articles—'Sub Specie Aeternitatis', dealing with the religious aspects of the war (No. 10) and 'A Philosophy of Pacifism', devoted to a newly published book of Bertrand Russell. This latter culminated in the view that 'his *Principles of Social Reconstruction* are a philosophic failure: the psychology of his pacifist politics is vague and wrong, and so is its ethical foundation. The principles of the "Principles" are lacking.'

Good examples of his critical attitude are provided by the following 'Autograph Notes', which he sent to me on the eve of publication, but which for one reason or another never actually appeared in print.

XVII—Notes

[Intended for *New Europe*, 8 October]

"*Peace Terms.*

Mr Trevelyan* is not right in supposing that all Socialists and the Chancellor are against annexation: Bethmann Hollweg put

* Now Sir Charles: at that time a prominent member of the Union of Democratic Control.

it very clearly that Germany must correct her Eastern frontier, and among the majority of German Socialists there are many who are annexationists. Mr Trevelyan's view seems to coincide with Professor Münsterberg of Harvard, who is agitating in U.S.A. for a drawn-game peace, which of course means the victory of Germany. Mr Trevelyan imagines that the restoring of independence to Serbia would be a very desirable peace term: we cannot agree with such a view. Serbia was independent before the war: Austria-Hungary and Germany would have left Serbia untouched, if she would have accepted Pan-German control. This is the question: whether Serbia shall be left to Austria-Hungary and her influence, and whether, therefore, the South Slavs shall be united. The restoration of Serbian independence cannot therefore be the real aim of the Allies. Mr Trevelyan seems to think that Constantinople should not become Russian: shall it be Turk? Then it is, in fact, German."

XVIII—Notes

[Intended for No. 2—24 October]

"*Signa Temporis.*

In the beginning of October there were some peace talks deserving of notice. The Kaiser spoke at the dinner given at the Mannheim Headquarters in honour of Marshal Hindenburg's 69th birthday. The speech was short. In the first place the Kaiser himself was put forward as the Supreme War Lord, then God was mentioned twice and mankind was informed that the Central Powers are fighting for freedom. A much longer speech is to be recorded of the Crown Prince. He chose an American clergyman, Mr Hale, the representative of Mr Hearst in Germany. The utterances of the Crown Prince were utterly disgusting, the falseness too transparent. The press of all Allied and neutral countries unanimously repudiated it. 'We are all tired of bloodshed, we want peace, etc.' Everyone knows that the Crown Prince was one of the staunchest advocates of the war. Everyone remembers how he applauded Heydebrand's challenge in the Reichstag. But the speech is not only characteristic of the bad taste of the German Crown Prince, but also of the political and strategic situation.

At the same time Prince Alexander of Hohenlohe is reported to have appealed to the Pope and President Wilson to step in and conserve European civilisation, even at the eleventh hour, from utter ruin. Prince Hohenlohe expects there will be no victory on either side, only a drawn game.

The true answer to this peace talk is given by M. Chéradame, whose book we have reviewed in another column. There it is explained what the drawn game means, and Prince Hohenlohe is wrong in assuming that the unprecedented courage and perseverance and firmness of the Allies give Germany equal rights. No: if the Allies are fighting as well as the Germans, and this is in fact readily acknowledged and admitted by the Germans, then it means that Germany is defeated. Germany prepared the war for many years, she organised her tremendous militarism, and now it is proved that nations which have not prepared for war, and do not have militarism, can stop the German offensive and fight no worse than the military specialists."

* * *

As further examples of his method may be added the following extracts from a series of 'Marginal Notes', which he sent me as they occurred to him. In this connection he went out of his way to write: 'Respecting my contributions to *New Europe*, it is a matter of course that you can dispose of them as you like—omit, complete, etc.'

XIX—Notes intended for *New Europe*.

"*Notes on* LLOYD GEORGE'S *first speech as* PRIME MINISTER

1. The whole programme is *administrative* only: he did not give a *political* programme. Perhaps this is quite good for England: to emphasise the necessity of national organisation.

2. The (short!) German Peace Note emphasises *three times* that Germany has been forced to this war: an adequate 'answer' to

the note should have shown that this assertion is false. That must be *proved*—a bare counter-assertion is not sufficient.

3. Perhaps the political programme is reserved for the common answer of the Allies.

4. Lloyd George used a very strong expression about Roumania ('blundered'): the blunder is on the side of the Allies, who allowed the Roumanian 'blunder'.

5. Passage on Greece—unclear: the 'agents' of Venizelos will be 'acknowledged'! not Venizelos!

6. The answer given by Lord Robert Cecil to a questioner is also unclear: he speaks of the *fact* of two Governments: but the question is about their *right*! That a deputy can acquiesce in such an evasive answer!

Résumé. Lloyd George's speech was excellent, it shows that the Prime Minister is wholly occupied by the *administrative* problem. These are the means to an end. This end must be cleared up also. Will Balfour do that on a given occasion? or Lloyd George himself?

On WILSON'S NOTE *to the* BELLIGERENT GOVERNMENTS (Dec. 1916)

Not clear.

1. His Note not associated with the German 'in its origin': but he recommends to consider it with 'other' peace proposals. There is only *one*—the German—proposal.

2. The objects of the war are virtually the same? But he himself says (and in that he is right), that the 'concrete objects' have never been definitely stated.

3. Very dangerous and absolutely unacceptable is the view that the issues of the war must first be settled 'upon terms which will certainly safeguard the independence, the territorial integrity and the political and commercial freedom of the nations involved'.

Status quo ante? = German Peace!

4. What are the 'smaller and weaker peoples'? He speaks of 'weak peoples and Small States'.

How can the liberty of smaller nations be secured without *territorial* changes? Will he force Prussia to give up her Germanisation in Posnania?

'Territorial integrity': how is it with Poland? If Russia must give up her Polish territory, what of the Austrian and Prussian Polish territory?

Résumé. Absolutely unclear.

Confirmed by Lansing's answer.

On AUSTRIA-HUNGARY

The Germans are not better than the Magyars: they cannot use the army as the Magyars do, but they do all to secure their majority. In Bohemia, South Styria, etc. (in Vienna!) they threaten the Slav minorities in every way possible. One sees in Posnania what the Germans are capable of, and so they will act in Austria. 'Kill with kindness'—the Magyars kill without kindness.

A Life and Death Struggle

1. £700,000,000 is a success: but
   (*a*) Germany had equal successes.
   (*b*) £700,000,000 covers the expenses of *about three months* only, for a part of the money is already spent (= the expenses must be covered by this loan).

2. Thoroughgoing economy is necessary. A Committee should be created to work out a scheme for making the administration more effective and cheaper. The Empire policy now aimed at presupposes reform of the whole administrative machinery.

3. The question which country is richer, Great Britain or Germany, contains two considerations:
   (*a*) Great Britain is richer in the sense of accumulated wealth: her colonies and industries are older than the German.

(*b*) The Germans have more hands—68 as against 43 millions. German industry (*a*) is more effective, (*b*) is better organised, (*c*) uses its scientific achievements better.

4. Struggle for life and death not only at the front, but at home as well.

(*a*) Output of shells, guns, ships, etc.
(*b*) Economy of food and home economy in general.
(*c*) Economy in state administration.

5. Lloyd George. All his speeches testify that his brain is absorbed by the administrative problem: but there must be also a vivid consciousness of the political aims of the war: without clear political aims the best administration, and even strategical victory, will be nullified.

On WILSON'S IDEAS

In fact Wilson accepts the programme of the Allies: Regeneration of Europe and Mankind, or Peace and Justice.

This can be attained by five means, which he proposed:

1. Every people is free to determine its own polity.
2. Avoid entangling alliances. Not a new balance of power, but a community of power = *lasting* peace.
3. Government by the consent of the governed.
4. Freedom of the seas.
5. Moderation of armaments.

Though he does not say it, his principles demand the acknowledgement of a sound principle of nationality.

He gives Poland as an instance (some papers write as if he demanded only Poland!) and

He says: 'united, independent and autonomous' (i.e. Posnania and Galicia are demanded).

Wilson's scheme is an attempt to formulate the principle of a truly democratic state and Government.

He has tried to formulate this in his writings. Take for instance his best-known essay, *Mere Literature*: but previously to that, in his book on *The State* one finds almost all that he says in his Note. And very interesting is his book *Congressional Government*, showing how in America democracy is eluded by the strong leaning towards centralism: Congress absorbs the federal states, and in Congress the Committee is assuming the highest power.

Having written such books, Wilson should have spoken still more concretely: I mean, to be understood by the masses, who have no time to read his books and ponder every word.

In his book on *The State*, for instance, he demands the freedom of Bohemia: he says that Bohemia *at least* must get the same independence as Hungary, having the same right.

We asked the Allies to speak clearly: they can ask the same from him.

Be sure and quote Balfour's dispatch: Balfour must not be pushed either to our opponents. He asks for a clearer statement. He denounces clearly Prussianism and advocates the Principle of Nationality, and he accepts the map of the Allies.

America's Decision

1. So far the moral effect is to be booked to the advantage of the Allies: the greater in that Wilson is (*a*) a kind of pacifist, and (*b*) a democrat.

Wilson's decision is a proof that no honest country can accept German *principles*.

2. People philosophise as to what Germany means in threatening America so insolently?

(*a*) To be forced to peace, to have an excuse that the whole world is against Germany and that she cannot stand, but that such a defeat equals victory in fact.

(*b*) To prevent America supplying ammunition to the Allies.

(*c*) To be able to invade Denmark (there are rumours that this is Germany's intention).

(*d*) If Germany gives in, she will do it to have an argument against Tirpitz, Reventlow, etc."

* * *

On 15 October Masaryk asked that steps should be taken to procure a visa for Mr Vojta Beneš (brother of the future President Beneš), to go to France and return to England on his way to America. At the same time he enclosed a translation of the latter's report on the counter-espionage activities of Emanuel Voska, which deserves inclusion.*

XX—Report of Vojta Beneš to T. G. Masaryk

London, 29 October 1916.

"Dear Professor,

In compliance with your request I submit a report on the work of Mr E. Voska, and the co-operation of the Bohemian National Alliance in the question you have suggested to me.

I regret that my report is not sufficiently complete and accurate in some points. During the last two years there has been so much of this work that it is impossible to reproduce all of it from memory. Apart from that, in many of Mr Voska's actions I had no active part, but they were related to me afterwards by Mr Voska. All these are just confidential questions, and as soon as I return to the United States I shall send a detailed report.

The work was mainly of two kinds:

(1) Confidential. (2) Propagandist.

The confidential work was done exclusively by Mr Voska. It was he who reported to the British authorities a number of cases of Austrian, German, etc. spies, officers, etc., who tried to get from America to Germany by different routes, and generally the names of persons, businesses, banks, etc. dangerous to the Allies. He gave the purpose of their mission, the names of the ships and

* See *Spy and Counterspy*, by Emanuel Victor Voska and Will Irwin (1941)—a rather sensational and not very reliable record.

the dates of sailing, photographs, etc. Acting on his information the British authorities captured these dangerous individuals and spoiled their work. Among those captured were, for instance, Lynar, Archibald, etc.

Mr Voska gained possession of the documents by means of which he detected the activities of von Papen, Boy Ed* and compromised the Ambassador Dumba.

These great political conspiracies, by which the official participation of Austria-Hungary and Germany in the crimes against American munition industries have been ascertained, have been exposed solely by Mr Voska.

This revelation was made public in the *Providence Journal*, under the name of the late Austrian Consul, Dr Goričar.† But Dr Goričar was only used as a blind, so that the true source of these revelations, so compromising to Austria-Hungary and Germany, might remain unknown.

Mr Voska's revelations had an immense influence on public opinion in America. The German propaganda, working purposefully, and being well organised by the aid of many millions of dollars, met with great success in its attempt to capture public opinion in the United States, even the catastrophe of the *Lusitania* having failed to affect it.

The pro-German party grew in numbers. Inspired and well-paid journalists writing in English, as well as in other languages, were either pro-German or neutral, and America was inundated with German pamphlets. The Society of the Friends of Peace increased in numbers, an indifferent neutrality became ever more apparent, and the agitation against the munition industry grew daily more pronounced.

And then came Mr Voska's revelations. German millions were discovered to be behind an action which clearly proved the connection of Austria-Hungary and Germany with the criminal attempts which destroyed American lives and property, and

* The German Military and Naval attachés at Washington.
† A Slovene by birth.

greatly injured the prestige of the United States at home. That was a thing which stung public opinion cruelly, and greatly reduced the effect of German propaganda.

Further revelations with regard to the Austro-Hungarian Ambassador Zwiedineck in the affair of the corruption of the Slav and other press in the United States are again the work of Mr Voska. The Austro-Hungarian Government gave millions to propaganda, and it was particularly interested in corrupting the press of the Slav nations of Austria-Hungary in America, and in trying to gain their favour. These efforts met with scant success, but in the few cases where they succeeded Mr Voska came forward and unmasked them. Thus even the undecided elements among the Slavs became less reliable. Recently Mr Voska convicted some Polish journals of having been corrupted [*name is given*].

These proofs of the base activities of the German and Austro-Hungarian Governments had an enormous influence on another question—on the question of munitions.

On the first attempt of the pro-German party to stop the export of munitions Mr Voska, by his prompt interference, was able to prevent its endeavour to provoke strikes in the munition industry. The fact that the conference of the leaders of the workmen, which took place in Atlanta, refrained from resorting to a strike was entirely due to the influence of Mr Voska, who is well known in these circles.

Hammerling's* attempt to gain over a league of the non-English press for the purpose of stopping the export of munitions was prevented among the Bohemians by the influence of the Bohemian National Alliance.

As the agitation of the pro-German Society of the Friends of Peace was becoming very serious, I wrote a pamphlet against it. The pamphlet was translated and published in seven languages, and distributed in the munition factories of all the great industrial

* A prominent German-Jewish agent of the German Government in the United States.

centres. Great meetings of workmen in the munition centres of Bethlehem, Bridgeport (Con.), Cleveland, Pittsburg, were held, where Mr Voska, Mr Getting (a Slovak) and I spoke against the Austro-Hungarian propaganda. Thus we were able to influence the workmen immediately, and with excellent results.

The Austro-Hungarian Ambassador, Constantin Dumba, requested the Bohemian and other papers to publish an official warning (for which they were to be well paid) to the workmen of Austro-Hungarian origin that, under dire penalties, they were not to accept employment in munition factories. As a result of our counter-propaganda, and by the influence of the Bohemian National Alliance, not only the Bohemian journals, but the rest of the Slav press, with very few exceptions, refused to publish the announcement: on the contrary, the Bohemian press denounced these threats very strongly. When Ambassador Dumba tried afterwards to justify his actions by a declaration concerning the want of culture of the Slav peoples, the Czechs and Slovaks arranged numerous meetings all over the United States, in which they clearly and explicitly condemned the immoral propaganda of Germany and Austria-Hungary. Subsequently a great number of petitions in that sense were sent to the President of the United States from all quarters.

When continuous attempts were being made in New York to prevent the export of sugar to England and many ships were destroyed, Mr Voska undertook to provide inspectors and watchmen from among our people, and thus, to a great extent, put a stop to further damage.

As regards propaganda, the Bohemian National Alliance worked partly by arranging meetings, partly through the Anglo-American press, as well as by the distribution of pamphlets. Hundreds of meetings have been held in the United States against the Central Powers, in which the American public were given an explanation and a description of the Pangermanic plan and its weapons, and we published reports and articles on this question in hundreds of the most serious of the Anglo-American journals.

Mr Voska and I distributed upwards of 20,000 pamphlets and leaflets (which were sent to us mostly from London) all over the United States, sending them according to a definite plan to prominent addresses, schools and libraries (articles on the case of Miss Cavell, on the *Lusitania*, Germany and Eastern Europe, Poland, etc.).

I have achieved this object, that the Bohemian Socialists in America accepted my proposal and wording of a manifesto to the International, in which they declared themselves against the Central Powers and in favour of the Allies. The Bohemians were the first among the workmen of the United States to declare themselves against the summary statement—which took root owing to German influence—that this war is a capitalistic war, and that it is the duty of the American workmen to do their utmost to stop this war of militaristic capitalism.

The Bohemian Manifesto, and after it the Manifesto of the South Slav Socialists, was the first blow to this German theory, and to-day, owing to it, the point of view of the American working classes is divided, and the workmen's campaign against the export of munitions has been considerably weakened.

That is all that I am able to say in the meantime. As soon as I return I shall go through all the cases of Mr Voska's work, and shall then submit a more exact report.

I am, very respectfully, V. B."

* * *

During the early months of 1917 all else was overshadowed by the Russian Revolution, soon to be followed by America's entry into the war. Already on 20 March Masaryk wrote to me that he must get to Petrograd as soon as possible: and steps were taken through the Foreign Office and Scotland Yard to arrange his journey. This time he travelled no longer on a Serbian, but a British passport, and it was Sir Basil Thompson, head of the C.I.D., who—for reasons that I never quite discovered—recommended him to use the name of Marsden. At the last moment he was recalled from the North Sea port from which he was to sail:

Štefaník had just arrived back from Russia, with urgent messages for him. The delay was providential, for the ship was sunk by a German U-boat two days later. The ship on which he eventually sailed for Norway was missed by a torpedo, literally by a few yards. The Provisional Government, which he found in power, was very largely recruited from his political friends; but unfortunately the one on whose help he most relied, Milyukov, was already on the point of resigning from the position of Foreign Minister.

This is not the place to tell the romantic story of Masaryk in Russia, of the way in which an elderly professor of philosophy organised the Czech Legions as the germ of a new army, ran the gauntlet of civil war and commotion, and finally withdrew across Siberia with his men, defying the Bolshevik Government, which sought to disarm them, and helping themselves to food, munitions, and even armoured trains—in fact, all that was necessary to maintain the army in transit and bring it safely to Vladivostok.

Masaryk was as anxious as we were to maintain and strengthen our contacts with Liberal Russia, and in the name of our group he was to offer the columns of the *New Europe* to representative writers of the new regime. Already on 24 March 'Marsden' sent me a telegram containing the four words 'Adler's analysis of Austria'. On 18 October 1916 Friedrich Adler, the Austro-Jewish Socialist leader, had deliberately assassinated the Austrian Premier, Count Stürgkh, as one of those most responsible for the war; and the speech which he now delivered in his own defence before a Viennese court was a reasoned indictment of the whole political regime in Austria. Masaryk's telegram meant that in his opinion—and he was in no way exaggerating—this speech was a revealing human document, containing the very quintessence of the Austrian problem as a whole, and should be presented thus to readers of the *New Europe*.

Unfortunately it soon became clear, long before the Second, or Bolshevik, Revolution threw our friends from power and soon developed into a bloody chaotic civil war, that communications between London and Moscow were virtually impossible. The following letter, the last which reached me from Russia, shows this.

XXI—Masaryk to Seton-Watson

Petrograd, Moraskaya 17, 24. vi. 1917.

"Dear Mr Seton-Watson,

There is almost no communication between Russia and England: for instance, I have had no letter since I came here, only telegrams. Russia is isolated from England and France, but not from Germany: a better communication between the Allies would have political influence. The *New Europe* is almost unknown: now and then people get a copy, but nobody has the whole series.

So far I did not succeed in finding the collaborators for *New Europe* whom you wished to have. I am trying to start a Russian New Europe: Shakhmatov and Milyukov are at the head of the committee working in that direction. If we succeed, then there will be a staff of collaborators, and among them there will be some for *New Europe*. Yet I do not expect that they will write many articles for us.

I send you to-day the Memorandum of the (Austrian) Southern Slav officers. It is a very serious matter. I spoke with some of the men: they explained their anti-Serbian attitude (among other reasons given in the memorandum itself) by the fact that Supilo and Vošnjak (?)* left the Committee. It seems to me the Committee is too passive: as there are in Russia so many prisoners, it would be of great value if the Committee would work among them. There is no doubt a very energetic Austrian and Magyar propaganda among the South Slavs.

M. Spalajković † told me that General Živković ‡ is going to

* A Slovene member of the exiled Jugoslav Committee. The rumour was false, both as regards him and Supilo.

† Serbian Minister in Petrograd, afterwards Jugoslav Minister in Paris, tinged with Pan-Serb sentiments.

‡ A Serbian Staff Officer, sent to command the Jugoslav Legions in Russia.

publish a counter-memorandum (Spalajković will be removed, I hear, and replaced by the Minister to the Vatican). And I read in the papers that the Southern Slav Committee will meet in Corfu: this geography kills the work.*

I have no idea when I shall be able to come to London. There is no longer any disorder in our Bohemian and Slovak ranks. The revolution helped us by checking the reactionaries. But the slowness of the administration will detain us longer than is really necessary. We agreed (the Russian and French Governments) to form a Bohemian (and Slovak) army of about 30,000 for France —though it is very difficult to put this into practice.

As I am not quite sure whether the letter, though sent by courier, may not be lost, I do not write much. There will be time to use my information and experience after my return.

Yours, T. G. MASARYK.

I hope you have got Iliodor's book on Rasputin; it must be used with caution, but Mr Leeper will understand not only Rasputin, but Iliodor † also."

* * *

My next news of Masaryk came from the other side of the world.

XXII—MASARYK TO SETON-WATSON

Sunday, 31 March 1918

"Dear Mr Seton-Watson,

I am on the way to London, approaching Vladivostok: I shall stay some days in Tokyo, and of course in the States, in order to visit Washington. I hope to be in London in the second half of May.

I write only what seems to be necessary at this moment, postponing the rest and all details for the final report to you and our friends in London.

* This time there was a good result—the Declaration of Corfu of 25 July 1917, which may be regarded as the foundation charter of the future Jugoslavia.

† Mr Rex Leeper had published a number of articles on the Russian Revolution in the *New Europe*, writing under the pseudonym of 'Rurik'.

I begin, then, with introducing to you and Mr Steed Major John K. D. Fitzwilliams: I made his acquaintance in Kiev. He is the chief of the British Military Mission: we agreed on many points, and I hope he may have some influence at the War Office. Perhaps he may be a little afraid of the Press and its representatives, but that is rather the inculcated view of soldiers who have been away from England. He will come to see you and you will inform him about the *personal* situation—through whom to act.

I mention also Lady Muriel Paget: she did good Red Cross work in Odessa, etc.

The first and foremost duty of the Allies now is to frustrate in every possible way a German Peace with Russia, and that can be done by not allowing the Russian (and Ukrainian) grain to be brought to Germany. There are two ways of achieving this aim.

(*a*) The organisation of a company to buy, sell and store the grain. No expense: the capital invested would be recovered.

The Russian peasant will not take money for his grain, for he cannot buy anything for it: he expects manufactured goods—all kinds of useful things, such as clothes, boots, soap, tools, nails, hatchets, agricultural machinery, and so on.

Now is the best occasion for foreign industry to become known and accepted by the Russian peasant: the Germans at present have no such industry.

I shall propose this plan to our American friends, and shall speak with the Japanese also—the principal thing is to prevent the grain going to Germany or Austria: it is of no importance now as to who will be the first to perform the task.

Major Fitzwilliams has an excellent man who could be at the head of such a business—Mr Howe, an English mill-engineer, who knows Russia and in particular the grain trade: he is returning to England with us.

(*b*) There is also a radical method of dealing with the German exportation of Russian grain—grain-terrorism: to annihilate the stocks. Of this I will tell you more in London.

(*c*) Coming to political questions, I am in favour of acknowledging the Bolshevik Government: once on good terms with the men, the Allies would be able to influence them. I know there is much talk about the supposed German plan to restore the Monarchy: but the fact remains that the Germans concluded peace with the Bolsheviks and thereby acknowledged their authority. That the Bolsheviks know and take into account. Perhaps the British Government would not like to acknowledge the Bolshevik regime without reserves: but it would be easy to find the appropriate diplomatic formula.

(*d*) By proposing this acknowledgement I express my conviction that the so-called monarchical movement (especially on the Don) is a *quantité négligeable.* I cannot write on that matter, but I know all about it: Major F. knows things too, partly from his own experience. He agrees with me. It is a great mistake to expect from the Monarchists, and even from the Cadets, real positive, constructive, political work.

(*e*) The Bolshevik regime will last longer than its opponents expect: if monarchism is to be restored, it will have to pass through some Socialistic coalition: monarchism restored at once, by force, would be of no great use for the Allies. The Allies must look to the future: not to be lost in the moment! Again, remember William concluded peace with the revolutionists and terrorists! And above all, the Allies must have a real interest in Russia's development, a sincere interest.

(*f*) A weak Russia is the greatest aid for a German Central Europe and Central Africa: the Allies must work for Russia on a grand scale, aid Russian development by all means (railways, etc.).

(*g*) By the way: a Russian army (*army*, not guerilla detachments) cannot be formed in less than 6–9 months: the Bolsheviks are inviting (ex-) officers as 'instructors': but there will be no efficient army without railways and industry.

(*h*) The Allies must learn to exercise more influence upon Russian public opinion. The Germans have been working since the beginning of the war and have even doubled their energy: the German prisoners scattered all over the country influence all kinds of local papers, and of course they have their unseen hand in the Petrograd press also.

This influence on local papers is of great importance! I would have a scheme of counteraction—to use our Bohemian officers. To some extent this work is already being done.

(*j*) All proposals converge upon an energetic demand for organised Unity of Action by all the Allies. There is a sad story to be told about the divergence of opinions and doings! And on things of the greatest importance!

(*k*) This unity of action in Russia of course presupposes that the Allied Governments have a clear plan and decided opinions: their Embassies and Consulates must not be left without directions!

(*l*) Finally, some words about our Czechoslovak Army:

(*a*) In Russia. I succeeded in forming a corps of about 50,000 men: the Allies (not only the French) agreed to support this army and bring it to Europe.

No doubt the expenses are comparatively high: but it is the political significance which is important. I know of course that there are many Austrophils, and that Austria is playing the anti-German card: but she does all that the Germans demand of her. The Allies can weaken Germany by abandoning Austria: they must not strengthen Berlin-Vienna by granting in advance to Austria her odious domination over the various nations. No sensible buyer will praise the seller's goods before buying them!

Therefore—the Allies must procure the necessary ships for our men.

(*b*) But we shall form a second corps of about 50,000 men, to prevent our prisoners being sent to Austria and the Italian battlefields.

(*m*) In general, the Allies should have a clear prisoner policy. It has been, and still is, possible to influence the prisoners: the Germans worked very hard in this direction from the very beginning, and they are still trying, not only in Germany but in Russia also. The Allies missed their opportunity in this as in many other matters.

I will speak about these things in Washington, with due discretion, of course, so as not to prejudice the Americans against their allies. Please show this letter to Mr Steed and Madame Rose, and to my daughter.*

Goodbye, yours, T. G. MASARYK.

N.B. I found here among unofficial people some Englishmen (I mean Britishers in general), who know Russian quite well and have a sound judgment on political matters: among the official men I found a naval officer—Mr **** of the Intelligence Department, who is an excellent observer and very clever man. He is at Kiev (if he did not leave at the German invasion). Don't forget Mr Webster: he could be of use to the *New Europe*.

P.S. 27 April 1918, written on R.M.S. *Empress of India*.

I have been delayed. There was no boat in Vladivostok for Japan, so I had to go via Harbin-Fusan and I had to stay in Japan until the 20th.

I enclose here some copies of documents which will give you a better idea of what I have written in Siberia.

(*a*) The American Ambassador in Tokyo had been informed from Washington about my arrival, and asked to put me some questions: I answered these, and wrote the enclosed abstract of them, which has been wired to Washington.

(*b*) Not only the French, but the Allies, are interested in our soldiers.

(*c*) Our soldiers have not only the way through Siberia, they could also use Archangelsk and Murmansk.

(*d*) Shows that one can come to an agreement with the Bolsheviks.

I shall be in Vancouver on Monday the 29th, in Chicago on 3 May: I do not know how long I may have to stay in the States, but I will try to come to London as soon as possible.

* Olga—now Mme Révilliod.

I wrote a little book on the War, which I hope can be published in Chicago or New York:* in London or Paris I shall try to publish the Atlas about which we spoke. The war has been prolonged, there is time to publish it, and it is necessary, as I see. I cannot speak about the War and the Allies, as I had no news. The situation is serious.

Yours, T. G. M."

ENCLOSURE A (referred to in letter above)

(10 April 1918)

"1. The Allies should recognise the Bolshevik Government (*de facto*—the *de jure* recognition not to be discussed); President Wilson's message to their Moscow meeting was a step in this direction: being on good terms with the Bolsheviks, the Allies can influence them. The Germans recognised them by concluding peace with them. (I know the weak points of the Bolsheviks, but I know also the weak points of the other parties: they are neither better nor abler.)

2. The Monarchical movement is weak; the Allies must not support it. The Cadets and Social Revolutionaries are organising themselves against the Bolsheviks; I do not expect any great success from either of these parties. The Allies expected that Alexeiev and Kornilov would have a great success on the Don; I did not believe it, and refused to join them, though invited to do so by the leaders. The same applies to Semenov and others.

3. The Bolsheviks will hold power longer than their adversaries suppose. Like all other parties, they will die of political dilettantism. It is the curse of Tsarism that it did not teach people to work, to administer: the Bolsheviks have been weakened by their failure in the peace negotiations and in the land question, but on the other hand they are gaining sympathies because they are to work and because the other parties are weak.

* Eventually published in *The Making of a State*.

4. I am inclined to think that a Coalition Government (of the Socialist parties and the left of the Cadets) might win general support, though there would also have to be Bolsheviks in the Government.

5. A lasting democratic and republican Government in Russia will exercise (through the Socialists and Democrats) great pressure on Austria and Prussia; that is one reason why the Germans and Austrians are anti-Bolshevik.

6. All the small nations in the East of Europe (Finns, Poles, Esthonians, Letts, Lithuanians, Czechs, Slovaks and Roumanians), need a strong Russia, lest they be left at the mercy of the Germans and Austrians. The Allies must support Russia at all costs and by all possible means. If they conquer the East, the Germans will conquer the West.

7. A capable Government could induce the Ukrainians to be satisfied with an autonomous Republic, forming part of Russia; that was the original plan of the Ukrainians themselves. Not till later did they proclaim their independence, though in reality an independent Ukraine will be a German or an Austrian province. The Germans and Austrians are pursuing the same policy towards the Ukraine as towards Poland.

8. It must be remembered that the south of Russia is the rich part of the country, with fertile soil, the Black Sea and the Donetz Basin. The north is poor: Russian policy will gravitate towards the south.

9. The Allies must have a common plan for the best way of supporting Russia.

10. The Allied Governments must not leave their functionaries in Russia without instructions: in other words, they must have a clear Russian policy.

11. I hope the Japanese will not be against Russia; that would suit the Germans and Austrians. On the contrary, the Japanese should fight on the side of the Allies: the chasm between Japan and Germany would thus be widened.

12. Nowhere in Siberia did I see, between 15 March and

2 April, armed German and Austrian prisoners. The anarchy in Siberia is not greater than in Russia.

13. The Allies must fight the Germans and Austrians in Russia:

(*a*) By organising a company to buy up grain and sell it where it is needed: thus the Germans will be prevented from getting it. But the Russian and Ukrainian peasant will not sell his corn for money, because it is useless to him: he wants manufactured goods, such as boots, clothes, soap and tools. As the Germans and Austrians have no manufactured goods, the Allies have an excellent opportunity to get the Russian market. The plan only requires energy and organisation: the capital put in the business will be returned.

(*b*) German and Austrian agents will flock into Russia. Counter measures are necessary and must be organised. (American and other agents must bring samples and perhaps small 'travelling' exhibitions of selected goods together with illustrated catalogues.)

(*c*) The Germans influence the Russian press not only by their special journalistic agents, but through the German prisoners of war who write in the various papers all over the country, not only in the cities. To some extent our Czech prisoners work against this, but the whole thing needs organising.

(*d*) The Russian railways must be kept up: without railways there will be no army and no industry.

(*e*) The Germans have bought up Russian securities, so as to control industry in future.

(*f*) It is known that the Germans have influenced prisoners of war—for instance, by training Ukrainian prisoners for the Ukrainian army: the Allies could influence the German and Austrian prisoners as long as they remain in Russia, through the Press and special agents.

(*g*) I succeeded in organising in Russia out of our Czech and Slovak prisoners a corps of 50,000 men: I have agreed with the French Government to send it to France. The Allies can help to transport it: they are excellent soldiers, as they proved in the renewed offensive last June.

We can organise a second corps of the same size; that must be done to prevent our prisoners from returning to Austria, where they would be sent against the Allies on the Italian or French front. The Allies have agreed to provide us with the necessary means. In France we have a smaller corps also, partly sent from Russia, partly composed of our refugees; and I hope to be able to form one in Italy also.

The significance of having a whole Czech army in France is obvious; and I must acknowledge that France understood the political meaning of the matter from the very beginning, and supported our national movement in every way. Briand was the first statesman who publicly promised to our nation the help of the French Republic, and it was he who succeeded in inserting in the Allied Note to Wilson the explicit demand that the Czechoslovaks should be liberated. (The Czechoslovaks are the most westerly Slav barrier against Germany and Austria.) In present circumstances 100,000—nay even 50,000—trained soldiers may count a great deal.

14. My answer to the oft repeated question, whether an army could be formed in Russia, is that a million men could be raised in from 6–9 months. The Red Guard is of no use, and the Bolsheviks have already invited officers (of the old army) to join their army as instructors. For the army railroads are necessary.

Note: To-day's *Japan Advertiser*, 11th April, publishes the following news:

'*VOLUNTEERS LAY DOWN THEIR ARMS*

(The Czechoslovak Corps on its way to France, is intercepted by Trotsky.)

MOSCOW, April 5th—As the result of an understanding between M. Trotsky and the French Ambassador, the army of Slovak and Czech volunteers who were leaving for France surrendered its arms to the Soviet authorities. With the exception of General

Dieterichs, who was accompanying this corps to France, the officers have been dismissed.'

This is good news: the corps going to France needs no weapons, as it will be armed again in France; the officers mentioned are *Russian* officers who had joined our army."

* * *

MASARYK IN AMERICA

Read in May 1918, this letter and memorandum were too strong meat even for his friends in London, still more for the official world for which they were intended. Read twenty-four years later, they have a prophetic ring, and serve as a measure of his farsightedness and largeness of view. It was all the more remarkable in view of the obstacles which the Bolshevik authorities placed in the way of the Legionaries, but which in the end were triumphantly overcome. In 1941 the programme of Masaryk was being put into operation by Roosevelt, Churchill and Beaverbrook. In his memoirs Masaryk sums up in the downright phrase: 'It must unfortunately be recognised that the Allies had no Russian policy, and that their action against Russia was not united.' Another highly apposite quotation may be made from the same book. Masaryk closes his Russian chapter with the following two sentences: 'On 26 March the Moscow Commissar telegraphed to the local Soviets that the Czechoslovaks were not going through as an armed unit, but as free citizens, and that they carried a certain number of weapons as protection against the counter-revolutionaries. He added: "The Soviet of People's Commissars wishes every assistance to be given them on Russian soil."' The name of this Commissar was Stalin!

Masaryk had at first intended to press on to Europe, after a few brief visits to his compatriots in the United States. But he soon found himself engaged in absolutely decisive undertakings on the American Continent. The influence which he was able to exercise upon President Wilson came at the critical moment when the latter was supplementing the Fourteen Points by the

Four Principles. Masaryk has put on record his admiration for the 'manly and honourable' way in which Wilson revised his original views, especially with regard to Austria-Hungary. There can, however, be little doubt that the main instrument in effecting this change was Masaryk's own tactical skill, his marshalling of cogent arguments, and the care with which, in advance of his own decisive interviews, he primed some of the men whom he knew to enjoy great personal influence at the White House. A further factor, which played a much greater part than is generally realised, was the close alliance between Professor George Herron, one of Wilson's confidential 'mystery men' at Geneva, and Stephen Osuský, a young American-Slovak advocate whom Masaryk and Beneš had sent as Press Attaché to Switzerland, and whose special function it was to make contacts with Hungary and to watch and counter the various peace feelers of Austrian and Hungarian statesmen. It was upon ground prepared by these two men, in intimate collaboration, that the full futility of the secret overtures of the Emperor Charles and some of his advisers was brought home to the President.

By August the situation was ripe, and events began to assume a breakneck pace. At every stage Masaryk was ready for action. His discussions with Lansing, on the basis of the resolutions of the Roman Congress of Oppressed Nationalities; the recognition of Czechoslovakia as an 'Allied and belligerent nation', first by Britain on 9 August, then by America on 3 September; the Declaration of Independence launched by Masaryk from America on 14 October; the great Conference of Nationalities in Independence Hall at Philadelphia, at which Masaryk, Paderewski and Hinković were the most marked personalities—all these steps led up to the memorable exchange of Notes between President Wilson and Austria-Hungary. These Notes rapidly bore down the diplomatic defences of Vienna and Budapest, killed the Emperor's project of Austrian federalisation at birth, and wrested from him and his Governments recognition of Czechoslovak and Jugoslav Unity as an essential part of the foundation of the new settlement. The Dual Monarchy crumbled before the impact of Wilsonian diplomacy: and on 28 October Prague was the scene of a bloodless revolution, proclaiming the independent Czecho-slovak Republic. Next day the Jugoslav National Council at Zagreb, representing the seven million Jugoslavs of the Habsburg Monarchy, also threw off their allegiance. The Poles and Ruthenes had already seceded, and spokesmen of the Slovaks, Roumanians, and other nationalities in Hungary had publicly repudiated the claim of the Hungarian Parliament to represent them at the Peace Conference. Before the Austrian Armistice could be signed on 3 November at Villa Giusti Austria-Hungary, not merely as a Great Power, but as a state unit among the states of Europe, had already ceased to exist, and the signatures appended to the document had already lost their validity. And it was these events in the interior of the Monarchy which produced the final military collapse, not (as the grotesquely false Italian theory runs) the more or less imaginary victory at Vittorio Veneto, which produced the collapse. In one phrase, which can never be repeated too often or too emphatically, Austria-Hungary was not broken up by the Allies, Austria-Hungary broke down from within, and no one factor contributed more to this result than the Presidential thunderbolts.

Masaryk was still in America when the end came, and therefore crossed the Atlantic as President-elect, with the consciousness of having occupied a key position at the real moment of decision, thanks to his contacts, direct and indirect, with the White House.

On 29 November he arrived in London, and as his friends watched the train draw into Victoria station, and the Grenadier Guards paid him the royal salute, I could not help recalling that other arrival at a London terminus 3½ years earlier, when no one else knew what train he was coming by, and when we between us dragged his heavy trunk along the platform, because there were no porters to be found. The day before Steed and I had been asked to procure for the band of the Grenadiers the unfamiliar

IV. MASARYK AT LANY (1934)

music of the Domův Muj and the Tatra Hymn—the joint national anthem of the new Czechoslovak State. We succeeded in our task, but when the train drew in to the platform, we found that the band had very wisely substituted a spirited rendering of 'See the Conquering Hero comes'. After a brief interval, he went on via Paris and the Italian front, to his triumphant progress through the Republic which owed its resurrection so largely to his efforts.

In 1923 he returned to England on a brief visit, and found time to receive his Doctor's degree at Oxford. But he never carried out his longstanding project of a prolonged holiday in complete incognito, such as would enable him to explore the English and Scottish countryside in a way that was of course quite impossible under stress of war.

May this brief and unvarnished chronicle of Masaryk's years in exile serve not merely as a record of the past but as a pledge for the future—a future in which Britain and Czechoslovakia will follow common aims and ideals.

CHAPTER III

Independent Bohemia

(PROFESSOR MASARYK'S Confidential Memorandum of April 1915)

CONTENTS

Prefatory Notice.
The Aim of the Present War: Europe Regenerated.
The Modern Principle of Nationality.
West and East: the Small Nations.
Only three Great Nations in Europe: The Population Problem of the War.
The World Position of England and Russia: Sea Power and Land Power.
Germany: a Continental Power.
Bismarck's Policy towards Austria: Pan-Germanism.
Berlin-Bagdad.
The Dreibund as 'Drang nach Osten': Trieste, the Adriatic.
Austria, an Artificial State: her Progressive Dismemberment.
Bohemia as part of Austria-Hungary.
Bohemia forced to abandon Austria-Hungary.
Bohemia for Russia, Serbia and the Allies: Bohemia's share in the War.
Bohemia claims her Independence.
The Independent Bohemian State: Area and Population.
Possible Objections to the Creation of an Independent Bohemia: and Refutation of these Objections.

1 'It is difficult.'
2. Small States are strategically impossible.
3. The economic weakness of a small State.
4. Bohemian Landed Proprietorship.
5. The Question of National Minorities.
6. The Bohemian Minority in Vienna.

Bohemia not the only Nation to be freed.
Free Bohemia and Serbo-Croatia, as neighbouring Countries.
The Slavic Barrier against Germany's March to Constantinople-Bagdad.
This Slavic Barrier coincident with the Interests of the Allies in Asia.
Italy and the Slav Question: the Dalmatian Problem.
Bohemia and the Balkans: England, Russia and Germany.
Independent Bohemia: Constitution and Government.
A 'Sine qua non'.

INDEPENDENT BOHEMIA

Prefatory Notice

This Memorandum gives the programme for the reorganisation of Bohemia as an independent State.

It is the programme of all Bohemian political parties except the Catholic Clericals. All details and minor problems are omitted. The plan of reconstructing the independent Bohemian State in the very heart of Europe naturally leads to the fundamental political problems of the present war. The interdependence of all these problems explains why they are touched upon here, in so far as the Bohemian and Slav questions seem to require it.

These views are of course presented from the Bohemian standpoint; this will, it is hoped, facilitate an understanding of the Bohemian Question.

The Aim of the Present War: Europe Regenerated

British statesmen and politicians have frequently proclaimed as the idea and aim of this war the liberation and freedom of the small states and nations. The same principle has been proclaimed in France. In Russia the Tsar and the Generalissimo publicly spoke of the liberation of their Slav brethren, while in Britain and France the integrity of Belgium was specially emphasised.

In these solemn proclamations of the Allies the Regeneration of Europe was accentuated as an aim of the war.

The Modern Principle of Nationality

Till recently mankind was divided and organised into states and churches, without regard to Nationality. The modern era is characterised by the development of various nationalities, as strong political and state-forming forces.

In practice, language, as the medium of common cultural life and effort, is the main test of Nationality. Besides Nationality, in modern times economic development, as well as provident care for the masses—not merely for aristocratic minorities—has become a great political and racial force.

Nationality is not the only organising force in society, but it is a very powerful force, the more so as it is very often opposed to the State. The watchword 'National States' sums up the tendency of modern political development.

For the purposes of this Memorandum it is not necessary to estimate the degree to which Nationality works as a political power. The future may bring a decided victory of the organising power of Nationality; to-day it is at least well to recognise its force to the extent of avoiding the evils which have led to the war and have been revealed in its course.

West and East: the Small Nations

There is a striking difference between the west and east of Europe in regard to the composition of states and the number of small nations. The west has four (five) great nations and only five small ones, whereas the east has only one great nation and a great number of small ones. In the west the states are formed by one dominant race, in the east they are nationally mixed.

West

1. England	1. Portugal
2. France	2. Holland (and Flemings of Belgium)
3. Germany	3. Denmark
4. Italy	4. Norway
5. Spain	5. Sweden.

East

Russia, who herself includes many small nations, while Austria-Hungary is composed of nine nations, and the Balkans of seven nations.

Only three Great Nations in Europe: The Population Problem of the War

In fact there are only three great nations in Europe: Russia (170 millions), England (45 millions), Germany (65 millions).

These three are at least the greatest nations, measured by the number and the constant growth of population.

France was the greatest nation at the Congress of Vienna when Europe was shaped; Germany had in 1816 on the territory which she now possesses 27·8 millions; France more than 30. To-day France is much smaller than Germany and smaller than Britain.

Italy is the smallest of the greater nations; Spain will hardly be acknowledged as a great nation at all.

The difference in the growth of the population, the constant increase of it, the approximate determination of the period of doubling, the growing difference in the number of soldiers and workers, begin to instigate statesmen and politicians to regulate the migration of the population (emigration—immigration), and to pursue a far-sighted colonial policy.

The colonial effort of Germany and of France is to be looked at from this populationistic view; this view enables us to understand the antagonism of France and Germany, the alliance of France with Russia (170 millions), and the whole political situation of Europe.

The World Position of England and Russia: Sea power and Land power

The geographical position of England is unique; England is the Colonial and Sea Power *par excellence*; so far the only Sea Power, whereas Russia is the Continental Power *par excellence*. The modern means of communication at sea enable England to gather her colonial forces and even face the great army of continental Germany.

This difference and natural antithesis of England and Russia regulate the foreign policy and the military and naval character of the two States.

Both nations have a vital interest in Asia—hence the difference, but also the coincidence, of political interest displayed in the policy regarding Turkey, Persia, China, Japan, etc., and above all regarding Germany.

Germany: a Continental Power

The central position in Europe, the outgrowth and defeat of France in 1870, and the colonial endeavour bring Germany, with her large and dense population, into competition with Russia and England. Her military forces are directed against Russia, her navy against England.

Germany is essentially a continental Power. She is a military, not a naval, State.

Her central position induces Germany to arrogate the supremacy over Europe.

> Heeren, the great German historian and philosophic geographer, apprehended the future effect of uniting Germany at the Congress of Vienna: 'La constitution d'un État central de l'Europe ne saurait être indifférente aux puissances étrangères. Si c'était une grande monarchie quelle possibilité d'assurer la paix pour elle? Une telle puissance pourrait-elle résister longtemps à la tentation de s'arroger sur le reste de l'Europe la prépondérance à laquelle sa situation et sa puissance sembleraient l'autoriser? L'établissement d'une monarchie unique en Allemagne serait bientôt le tombeau de la liberté en Europe.'

Bismarck's Policy towards Austria: Pan-Germanism

As a Continental, overpopulated, Power Germany presses constantly on Austria and uses her. Bismarck's policy towards Austria is the diplomatic and political formulation of the constant pressure of the Prussian North on the Austrian South. Lagarde, the father of modern Pan-Germanism, formulated the German programme: 'Colonisation of Austria by Germany.'

By colonising Austria Germany aspires to colonise the Balkans and thus to reach Constantinople and Bagdad.

BERLIN-BAGDAD

This 'Drang nach Osten' explains the policy of Berlin towards the Magyars, towards Roumania, towards Bulgaria, and towards Turkey.

The watchword Berlin-Bagdad denotes the real aim of Germany, the direction of the 'Drang nach Osten'. The alliance with Turkey in the war is the final result of the German invasion in Constantinople and in Asia Minor (financial policy, railways, schools and hospitals, etc.).

> Known German politicians and publicists emphasise all the time during the war the plan to occupy Asia as far as Bagdad; for instance: Lamprecht, von Liszt, Dirr, the director of the Ethnological Museum, Munich, etc.

THE DREIBUND AS 'DRANG NACH OSTEN': TRIESTE, THE ADRIATIC

The Triple Alliance is the diplomatic and military weapon of the Berlin-Bagdad plan: Austria-Hungary is absolutely at Germany's disposition; Italy is checked in her national endeavour, for it is obvious that Germany tries to preserve Trieste and the Adriatic for herself—the way to Asia Minor and East Africa. The Pan-German politicians since Lagarde claim Trieste very strongly for Germany.

At bottom it is the German aspiration for Asia which reveals one of the most effective causes of the war and which explains the antagonism of Germany against England and against Russia.

Austria, an Artificial State: her Progressive Dismemberment

Austria, being an aggregate of nine small nations, is quite an artificial State, as she was called by an Austrian politician (Plener, the younger); no nation in Austria is so populous that it would have the ruling majority. The dynasty, therefore, tries to maintain its absolutistic position by the principle of *divide et impera*, by little concessions now to one nation, now to another; the Germans (the dynasty is German) and Magyars are the favourites.

Austria owes her origin to the invasions of the Turks, and previously of the Huns (Magyars); Austria means the Eastern Empire, the German provinces, Bohemia and Hungary joined in a federation against Turkey.

With the fall of the Turks Austria falls also; Austria lost her ruling idea, and is unable to find a positive idea.

So Austria falls from step to step. The Austrian-Spanish Empire was dissolved. Austria lost the greater part of Silesia and was driven by Prussia to abandon Germany; in 1848, saved by Russia, she lost in 1859 the Italian provinces; in 1866 she was beaten by Prussia. Since then she exists only as the vassal of Berlin, being divided into Austria and Hungary; it is to Berlin that both the Germans and Magyars owe their dominating position in Austria.

The other nations, especially the Bohemians and South Slavs, are in everlasting opposition against the two Prussified vassals, the Germans and Magyars. Austria was unable to unite all nations in a strong federation and to pursue her own aim to work for the growth and development of the single national components. Germany—and that is Bismarck's plan with Austria—uses the seeming Great Power for her own ends.

The war of 1914 has uncovered the weakness of the Dual Monarchy. Austria, though she initiated the war by her brutal and dishonest anti-Serbian policy, was not prepared for the war, was beaten by the Russians, lost the greater part of Galicia, and only the help of Germany and her strategical leading retards the final collapse.

Austria is degenerated, she is the Catholic Turkey, she has lost her *raison d'être*.

Bohemia as part of Austria-Hungary

Bohemia was formerly associated with German-Austria and with Hungary as an independent kingdom; the King was in common for all three States; each possessed its own administration. The revolution of 1618, leading to the battle at the White Mountain and causing the Thirty Years' War, did not deprive Bohemia of her independence; it was the absolutism of the eighteenth century, strengthened by the reaction against the French Revolution, which endeavoured to shape the three federated States into a centralised State. The revolution of 1848 in Hungary and in Bohemia restored the rights of Bohemia for a while; the reinforced absolutistic centralism was checked in 1859, and 1866. Vienna made peace with Hungary in 1867 (Dualism), but Bohemia had to continue to assert her rights and liberty. Since Vienna had to concede the Constitution, Bohemia and her legal representatives have been persistently fighting for independence against the German and Magyar supremacy.

In this fight she is supported by the non-German and non-Magyar nations, especially by the Southern Slavs.

Bohemia forced to abandon Austria-Hungary

The war of 1914 revealed, as did the two wars of 1859 and 1866, that Austria-Hungary is unable to protect and to administer Bohemia and the other nations. Vienna has utterly failed in this war, and failed the more, in view of the recent military preparations, since the annexation of Bosnia-Herzegovina; indeed, it was boastfully proclaimed that Austria-Hungary alone would defeat the Russians, the Germans directing their main forces against France and her Allies in the West.

Bohemia must now take care of herself.

Bohemia for Russia, Serbia and the Allies: Bohemia's share in the War

The Bohemians are since the awakening of the national feeling strongly Slavophil. The political meaning of Bohemian Slavophilism was revealed in 1849 by the summons of the Slav Congress at Prague, and later in the so-called Moscow Pilgrimage in 1876—Palacký himself, the 'Father of the Nation', manifested Russophil tendencies against Dualistic Austria.

In the last war of the Serbians and Bulgarians against Turkey the Bohemians, as is generally known, strongly helped the Slav Allies by sending physicians, sanitary materials, money, etc. Previously to that war the Bohemian representatives in the Delegation and in Parliament openly supported the Southern Slav cause against Vienna and Budapest.

Since the beginning of the war last August and its antecedents the Bohemian nation has manifested its sympathy for Russia, Serbia and the Allies.

Bohemia, as the majority of the belligerent nations, was surprised by the sudden, unexpected outbreak of the war; she was therefore not prepared to manifest her opposition to Vienna by a regular revolution; but she manifested her feelings and thoughts strongly enough.

Whereas representatives of the Germans, Magyars and Poles proclaimed their support of the war and their allegiance to the dynasty, the representatives of the Bohemians did not join in these proclamations; the Bohemians did not favour the War Loan, and it is known that Bohemian public opinion is constantly in conflict with the authorities, expressing sympathy with the Allies. It is further known that many Bohemian regiments only went to the front under compulsion, and that they showed their antipathy to the war by frequent demonstrations—reported in the papers—by declining to fight, and by repeated surrenders. There is documentary evidence that the Austrian Generalissimo fears this attitude of the Bohemian troops and civil population as a serious weakening of the Austro-Hungarian army.

Bohemia claims her Independence

All the Bohemian colonies abroad, especially those in Russia, England, France, Switzerland and the United States of America, not being under the pressure of Austria, have repeatedly manifested the true feeling of the nation, proclaiming the necessity of restoring the political independence of Bohemia. The official organ of political Bohemia abroad is *La Nation Tchèque*, appearing in Paris under the direction of Mr Ernest Denis, professor at the Sorbonne, the well-known historian of Bohemia.

To attain independence is the alleged aim of all Bohemia and of all political parties; there are only some few individual adherents of Austria. No politician of any repute is among them.

The Independent Bohemian State: Area and Population

The Bohemian State would be composed of the so-called Bohemian countries, namely of Bohemia, Moravia, Silesia; to these would be added the Slovak districts of North Hungary, from Ungvar through Kaschau along the ethnographical boundaries down the river Ipoly (Eipel) to the Danube, including Pressburg and the whole Slovak north to the frontier line of Hungary. The Slovaks are Bohemians, in spite of their using their dialect as their literary language. The Slovaks strive also for independence and accept the programme of union with Bohemia.

The Bohemian State would have a population of over 12 millions. The extent of the new state would be about 50,000 English square miles (Belgium has 11,373).

Possible Objections to the Creation of an Independent Bohemia: Refutation of these Objections

Against the reconstruction of an independent Bohemia some objections will be made, perhaps not only by its adversaries. The principal objections may therefore be formulated and discussed.

1. At the root, perhaps, of all objections is the fear of new political formations in general. This fear is commonly expressed in the saying, 'It is difficult'.

Yes, it is difficult. Every new political creation is difficult—difficult will be the restriction of German militarism and the political consequences of such restriction, if logically carried out. In politics habits, and not only good ones, but bad ones just as well, rule humanity.

2. Very often the saying is repeated, that a small State is impossible, small nations cannot protect and support themselves.

The far-reaching problem of small nations has often been discussed. Here it must be emphasised that independent Bohemia would not be so very small. Regarding her population, she would hold in Europe the eighth place, only seven States being greater: fourteen would be smaller.*

Greater than Bohemia

England	Poland	Italy	Russia
Germany	France	Spain	

Smaller than Bohemia

Portugal	Belgium	Holland
Denmark	Norway	Sweden
Switzerland	Serbia	Montenegro
Bulgaria	Greece (Albania)	Turkey (European)

Bohemia has no sea (unfortunately, only in one of Shakespeare's plays), and that is a great drawback, no doubt (compare small Denmark and the rest of the sea-bordered countries).

In that respect Bohemia is not alone (Serbia, the Magyars, Switzerland), but the example of Switzerland shows that not only can political independence be preserved, but that modern means of communication enable even a landlocked country to have a flourishing industry.

If, therefore, it is urged that Austria is necessary for her nations,

* Austria and Hungary bring the number from twelve to fourteen.

that Austria, if it did not exist, would have to be created, one must say with Palacký that Bohemia was before Austria, and that she will be after Austria.

Austria was created as a confederation of smaller States in the Middle Ages, against the fierce Turks and Huns, and against the oppressive spirit of the age in general. Since the military spirit and oppressive propensities of nations have grown relatively weaker, and as there is some good hope that the war will bring about a longer time of peace (1870 was followed by a 45 years' peace), Bohemia can, during that time, relatively easily be consolidated.

The necessary protection against hostile neighbours free Bohemia can get from alliances with equally threatened neighbours or with friendly neighbours. Bohemia will be contiguous with Poland and Russia, and perhaps with Serbia.

3. Economically and financially Bohemia is acknowledged to be the 'pearl of Austria'—she will be as rich as she is now; she will be richer, because she will not have to support the economically 'passive' provinces of Austria.

Be it noted that the part of Austria which really pays its way consists of Bohemia (with Moravia, Silesia), Lower Austria with Vienna, North Styria, part of West Galicia (this latter only in recent years).

Bohemia, of course, would take a part of the Austrian public debt, and as the war will augment this debt very greatly, Independent Bohemia would have to begin her own administration with a considerable burden: the leading political men of Bohemia are aware of this serious task, and of the necessity for a solid, thoroughly balanced financial administration.

4. In this outline it is impossible to discuss all problems of Bohemia.

But it is of general interest to point to the peculiar position of the Bohemian landed proprietors (aristocracy). These proprietors, for the most part, are Austrian in sentiment, and perhaps they would form a dangerous element. In their case Bohemia could follow the English example in Ireland (land purchase).

5. As it is not in our intention to hide the difficulties of Free Bohemia, we must mention the question of national minorities.

First, though we advocate the principle of nationality, we wish to retain our German minority. It seems to be a paradox, but it is on the principle of nationality that we retain the German minority. Bohemia is a quite unique example of a mixed country; in no country are two nationalities so intermixed and interwoven, so to say, as in Bohemia. Between the Germans and Italians, for instance, the ethnographical frontier is simple, sharply cut; it is not so in Bohemia—in a great many places, and in almost all the cities, we have Bohemian (or German) minorities. The Germans object that the Bohemian minorities in North Bohemia, etc. are 'only' working men, people who live on German bread; this anti-social argument is obviously false; it misrepresents the process of industrialisation of Bohemia, which of course needs factory 'hands'.

In Bohemian Silesia the majority is Polish and German, in the Slovak districts there would be a Magyar minority.

6. In a more detailed programme the Bohemian minority of Vienna (about half a million!) would have to be discussed.

Here it must suffice to hint at the possibility of repatriating a great part of the Bohemian emigrants in a free, and therefore richer, Bohemia.

Bohemia not the only Nation to be freed

The difficulties of reconstructing Independent Bohemia will be smaller if we take the problem in its connection with the other difficulties, i.e. with the construction and reconstruction of Poland and Serbo-Croatia, and of course with the liberation of the French and Danes in Germany, with the solution of the Balkan and Turkish question, and with all questions agitating the world in this war. The attempt to solve these questions is the very aim of regenerating Europe. All these questions together form the European problem.

Free Bohemia and Serbo-Croatia, as neighbouring Countries

The maximum of Bohemian and Serbo-Croatian wishes would be the connection of Bohemia and Serbo-Croatia.

This can be effected by giving the strip of land at the Hungarian frontier in the west either to Serbia or the half of it (north) to Bohemia, the other (south) to Serbia.

This corridor would be formed of parts of the counties of Pozsony (Pressburg), Sopron (Oedenburg), Moson (Wieselburg), and Vas (Eisenburg).

The population is German, containing considerable Croatian minorities; the south is Slovene.

As there are considerable Slovak and Serbo-Croatian minorities, which may be left to Hungary, it is not unjust to claim this district, the more so as the Magyars treated, and now treat, the Serbs and Croats in a way worthy of the Huns of the Middle Ages. Whole districts are depopulated, the inhabitants of Bosnia driven away to Montenegro, while those of Syrmia have been sent to Hungary, where they, not being cared for, die in masses. And the Slovaks were for centuries the victims of the most brutal Magyarisation.

The Serbo-Bohemian corridor would facilitate the economic interchange of both countries—industrial Bohemia and agricultural Serbo-Croatia—and it would lead from Bohemia to the Serbo-Croatian ports.

The corridor would, of course, have a great military significance.

It must be added that many Serbo-Croatian politicians accept this plan of a corridor, just as the Bohemian politicians.

The Slavic Barrier against Germany's March to Constantinople—Bagdad

By forming this Serbo-Bohemian corridor the Allies would prevent Germany from colonising the Balkans and Asia Minor, and they would prevent the Magyars from being the obedient advanced guard of Berlin.

This Slavic Barrier coincident with the Interests of the Allies in Asia

England as well as France once protected Turkey; that was unconsciously an anti-German policy, though it was directed against Russia, who protected the Balkan Slavs and nations. Now England and France have accepted the policy of Russia, while Germany has taken up the abandoned policy of the two Allies.

By protecting the Balkan Slavs and nations the Allies attain as much, and even more, than they attained by protecting Turkey, and they serve the cause of liberty and civilisation.

Logically the expulsion of Germany from Asia involves taking East Africa from her also. That is the direct consequence of the fall of Kiau-chau.

Italy and the Slav Question: the Dalmatian Problem

Only a few words must in this connection be said about Italy, and her exaggerated claims to Serbo-Croatian territory.

Italy overrates the possession of the Croatian coast (Fiume) and of Dalmatia. The command of the Adriatic will be secured by a numerous and good fleet, not by a poor and bare coast. Italy wishes the liberation of the Italians from the Austrian yoke, but at the same time she accepts the repudiated Austrian policy of national repression. Italy has to answer this question: Either she wishes to see in the Adriatic a strong Austrian and Turkish fleet and a German naval base at Trieste, Pola, or some place further south, or she must be at peace with Serbia, who until now has not had a single ship. Trieste, as an Italian *porto franco*, Pola, Valona, the islands in the Aegean, are more than sufficient for Italy's aspirations in Asia and Africa.

Of course Italy must consent to Russia having Constantinople and the Straits—if England and France have come to terms with Russia. Why should Italy pursue a Mediterranean policy based on a false idea regarding the Dalmatian coast?

This Adriatic policy is quite false, viewed from the present significance of the Mediterranean. This sea is now something different from what it was to the old Greeks and Romans: the free intercommunication of the countries bordering on this sea is not disputed, but to-day the Mediterranean leads these countries to Asia, Africa, Australia, America. England is a strong Mediterranean power, though only possessing two or three small places and one short coast line (Egypt). Does Italy, who has a very long coast of her own, and a number of islands (one of them is large), need the long coast of Dalmatia as well, if she gets Trieste, Pola and Valona?

Italy should remember that the old German Empire occupied Italian territory; the new German Empire will not hesitate to do the same, having already acquired a good deal of the industry in Northern Italy. The way to Bagdad goes from Berlin not only through Constantinople, but through Trieste and Venetia.

Italy is the natural ally of the Southern and Northern Slavs against the 'Drang nach Osten'.

Bohemia and the Balkans: England, Russia and Germany

Bohemia must wish that the Serbo-Croatian nation should be united and that Serbia should come to a satisfactory agreement with Bulgaria.

The Bohemian politicians hope that the final reconstruction of the Balkans will be solved in accordance with Russia and her

Allies. For Bohemia and the Balkan Slavs the friendship and help of Russia is essential.

The Bohemian politicians think that Constantinople, and therefore the Straits, can only belong to Russia. This is a long-cherished plan of the whole Russian nation; this plan has the religious sanction (Hagia Sofia!) of the Russian people, and it is the natural solution of the political and economic endeavour of Russia to secure the Black Sea and the free way to the Mediterranean and the Red Sea.

The Bohemian politicians rejoiced in the fact that Russia and England found each other and that the Persian question—(Persian Gulf!)—was solved. Russia, having Constantinople and the Straits, has no vital interest in the Persian Gulf and will be able to devote herself to the final incorporation of Constantinople.

Constantinople and the Straits mean a heavy administrative and financial burden, which only a Great Power will be able to support; Greece, Bulgaria, even in joining their efforts, would not be able to stand the task. It is to be hoped that both these nations will acknowledge this fact and accept its bearing on the final distribution of Asia Minor.

The Bohemian politicians hope and wish that Turkey will be wiped off the map. England is a greater Mohammedan power than Turkey. Russia nearly so: their agreement guarantees the future solution of the religious and political problems of the Mohammedan world. The Slavs are interested in this solution, for there are a good many Serbian and Bulgarian Mohammedans.

The Bohemian politicians set great value on the agreement of Russia and England, as they must fear that Bismarck's old policy of conciliating Russia will be revived by the war. It is not difficult to detect in many utterances of prominent German publicists and statesmen (among others of Hindenburg himself) a hidden appeal to Russia. The German designs in Asia at once suggest the immense significance of Russia as an Asiatic Continental Power. If the Germans also appeal to English Parliamentarism and Liberalism, the Bohemian politicians know that the Germans are blind adherents of the Prussian constitutional theory, which Treitschke formulated in the abstract, Bismarck practically, and to which the Kaiser lent sacrilegious expression, proclaiming the tool of Bismarck, his grandfather, as God's newest revelation.

Independent Bohemia: Constitution and Government

Bohemia is projected as a monarchical State; a Bohemian Republic is only advocated by a few Radical politicians.

The dynasty could be established in one of two ways. Either the Allies could give one of their princes, or there could be a personal union between Serbia and Bohemia, if the Serbo-Bohemian corridor could be formed.

The Bohemian people, that must be emphasised once more, are thoroughly Russophile. A Russian dynasty, in whatever form, would be most popular. At any rate, the Bohemian politicians wish the establishment of the kingdom of Bohemia in full accordance with Russia. Russia's wishes and plans will be of determinating influence.

The Bohemian politicians, knowing the difficult task of reconstituting Bohemia, do not shrink from the responsibility of the work to be done. If they wish complete independence, it is because they wish to use all the political forces of the nation to build a strong State. Not only Russia, but her Allies also, will be best served by strong Slav states and nations, and this aim will best be attained if these nations will bear the full responsibility of their policy.

Bohemia will, of course, be constitutional and democratic—as befits the nation of Hus, Chelčický and Comenius, the nation which was the first to break the mediaeval theocracy, and which by its reformation and fight for spiritual liberty prepared the modern development of Europe. It is this great service Bohemia has rendered to Europe and to mankind which gives her the right to claim her independence, and to have her seat and vote in the areopagus of free nations.

The regeneration of Europe will be attained not only by foreign policy, it must be chiefly attained by the active furtherance of liberty and progress in the inner life of the European nations. For this task the Allies can fully rely on the Bohemian nation.

A 'Sine qua non'

The presupposition of the Bohemian programme is the restriction of Germany and her defeat in this war.

This defeat must be twofold. First, it is the direct victory of the Allies over Germany; second, the lasting defeat of Germany will be the defeat of Austria-Hungary and the dismemberment of this artificial State. Every weakening of Austria is a weakening of Germany; Bismarck's plan of squeezing the Austrian lemon will be at an end.

To-day Germany disposes of the 50 millions of Austria's population; but after the non-German and non-Magyar nations have been freed, only 10 millions of these will be left—always assuming that German Austria remained on good terms with Germany, or even became incorporated.

Liberated Bohemia certainly will act in accordance with the Entente, and will always be a loyal ally to them; now Bohemia wishes and hopes that her Russian brethren will soon succeed in occupying the Bohemian and Slovak districts. This would be the best solution not merely of the Bohemian, but also of the Austrian, German, and other questions at issue.

CHAPTER IV

*The Problem of Small Nations in the European Crisis**

(The following is the text of PROFESSOR MASARYK's inaugural lecture to the School of Slavonic Studies, University of London, King's College. At the last moment the Prime Minister, Mr Asquith, being ill, his place was taken by Lord Robert Cecil, then assistant Foreign Secretary.)

INTRODUCTORY REMARKS

Your Excellencies, My Lords, Ladies and Gentlemen,

Your kind reception, I am aware of the fact and I rejoice at it, is due to the cause which I represent as lecturer at this new chair; I am deeply sensible of the honour conferred upon me by London University in asking me to give the inaugural lecture of the new school.

Like the audience, I deeply regret the illness which has prevented the Prime Minister from presiding to-day; I regret it all the more because I know what interest, on many occasions, he has shown in the welfare of universities and other educational establishments. In this case it is very significant that the head of the British Cabinet was willing to preside at a lecture on the problem of small nations; several members of the Cabinet and British Government have frequently proclaimed that the idea and aim of this European Crisis is the liberation and freedom of the small States and Nations. Mr Asquith's interest in these Slavonic studies is a good omen and an anticipation of what I shall bring forward in my lecture; I hope it even may be more, it may be a firm first step in the practical solution of the problem to be discussed.

In speaking thus I must not be suspected of confusing science with politics; but science is not to be regarded as something merely abstract and in the clouds; science means methodical and

* See Chap. II, pp. 72-3.

exact thought about everything within the range of human life. No honest man can avoid thinking about the war; science, according to a French thinker who was the living antithesis to militarism and even to politics, has to foresee, to know beforehand, to anticipate the future. The man of science does not give up his patriotism; but that patriotism cannot be blind or dumb; it must proclaim what he has found to be the truth. The highest aim of science is to understand the aims of life and to find the right means for realising those aims. Science, then, however theoretical it may be, inevitably exists in order to be carried into practice. In a word, true science, both in morals and in politics, directs and hardens the will. The will—for it is not enough for men to wish and to imagine that we are already exercising our will—to will in morals and politics presupposes clear seeing, understanding and knowledge. This at least in my opinion is the aim of our new School of Slavonic Studies; scientific work of this kind will help this country to understand not only the Slavs, but also herself.

I

1. It would help us greatly if I could show you a good map of the European nations; but no such map exists. This deficiency of ethnological geography is very significant of the scientific situation in this branch of sociological studies, which during this war, and as a result of it, has become so important. Still more significant is the fact that in spite of the war and the steady discussion of the different nationalities, you cannot buy a map showing the extent of the different nations; you will find political maps, maps of the railroads, etc., but no ethnographical ones. Think of it, the very question of the war is graphically not represented, though day by day for over a year past endless discussions, alike in the press and on the public platform, turn upon the question of nationality! Only a few specialists realise the situation and give us in their treatises and books a few all too scanty ethnographical data.

So inveterate is the conception of the *state* as the only social entity which counts in the political world. But to-day we are forced to acknowledge the existence of *nations* and we are obliged to make a distinction between states and nations; and that of course involves a true grasp of the incongruity of political and ethnographical boundaries. An Englishman, speaking of his nation, identifies the nation and the state. Not so the Serb or the Bohemian, because to his experience state and nation do not coincide, his nation being spread over several states, or sharing a state with other nations. We Slavs very keenly discriminate the state from the nation; but the Englishman will do the same if he uses expressions such as 'the spirit' or 'the culture' of the German and English nations.

In the *Statesman's Yearbook* for 1915 we find in Europe twenty-eight states, if we treat Austria-Hungary and Germany each as a single state; we must count fifty-three states, if we separate Hungary from Austria and divide Germany into her twenty-five federal units.

If we take one of the few better ethnological maps of Europe—alas, a German one—we find sixty-two nations or nationalities. In other words, in Europe we have more than twice as many nations as states, and that means that the existing states are nationally mixed, and that states must be composed of more than one nation. And that means further that there are in Europe far more dependent than independent nations. Only seventeen nations are independent, or rather possess their own state organisations; but portions even of these independent nations are dependent upon other states. In fact, there are only a few states which do not contain more than one nation—only seven out of the twenty-eight. But if there are seven national states, that does not mean that these seven states are formed by seven nationalities; for some states contain the same nationality, and in other cases the same nationality is divided among different states.

And be it noted at once, these national states (national in the strict sense of the word) are all small, some of them the smallest states. Andorra, Denmark, S. Marino, Liechtenstein, Monaco, Holland, Portugal. The Papal state in Rome belongs to a category of its own.

The middle-sized states, and still more the large states, are all mixed, though they vary in type according to the proportion, the numbers, and of course the cultural quality of the several units of which they are composed.

As a rule, one—the ruling—nation is in the majority; in different states this majority is differently scaled. But we have at least one instance where the minority tries to rule—the Germans in Austria, and, side by side with them, the Magyars in Hungary.

Austria-Hungary represents an unique type of the mixed or polyglot state: a comparatively high number of different smaller and small nations forms a single state. The Balkan federation, of which so many idealists, and even politicians, have dreamed, would of course belong to the same type.

2. For our present purpose it is not necessary to give an elaborate classification of the mixed states; any real sociological treatment of the subject requires exact description of the national units in each individual state; only then is fruitful comparison possible.

If we take the states directly involved in the war, we find that all of them are mixed, though in varying degrees. Germany, in addition to her sixty million German inhabitants, has six other nationalities, two of them in considerable numbers (Poles—Frenchmen); the other four, Lusatians (Sorbs), Danes, Czechs, Lithuanians, only forming tiny minorities. Austria-Hungary contains ten nationalities; Turkey-in-Europe, three and a few fragments of other nations in addition (Turks, Greeks, Bulgarians, Armenians, etc.; Asiatic Turkey is of course extremely mixed). Bulgaria is mixed, for there is a large Turkish minority, to say nothing of fragments of Roumanians, etc.

The states of the Allies are also mixed, but for the most part in a different manner. Great Britain has considerable remnants of non-English nations, and so has even France of races which are not French; even Italy, which is often proclaimed as an example of a national state, contains a few Slav, German and Albanian fragments. Serbia has non-Serbian minorities (Bulgarian and Albanian); even Montenegro, the smallest state, is mixed.

Russia is ethnologically an unique state: I speak of European Russia. The British Empire of course contains in its various trans-oceanic dominions and colonies many more nations and fragments of nations and races, but Great Britain is in the main English, whereas Continental Russia, though the Russians are in an overwhelming majority, contains many nations, of which several are numerous, and moreover nations which possess their own culture and traditions.*

3. Comparing the national composition of the European states we perceive a striking difference between the East and the West of Europe. If we bisect Europe by a line drawn from the Adriatic to the Baltic, and extended up to the head of the Gulf of Bothnia, we find in the West nineteen nations; nine are embodied in twelve states (Portugal, Spain, France, Italy, Holland, Denmark, Norway, Sweden, Germany, Great Britain, Belgium, Switzerland), the remainder are, in the main, national splinters.†

The state-nations in the West are of all magnitudes: a few great, some of medium size, and the rest small ones; there is a kind of national equilibrium.

The East of Europe offers quite a different spectacle. There we have one great nation—in fact the largest nation in Europe, the rest are all smaller and small nations, some few possessing independent states of their own. But in Eastern Europe—and this applies especially to Russia—we have a very great variety of national and racial fragments.

* On a special ethnographical map of Russia (Aïtoff, *Peuples et Langues de la Russie*, Annales de Géographie, 1906), one can enumerate eighty-five nations of some different races, and besides the author mentions nameless nationalities.

† Basques, Bretons, Welsh, Irish, Gaels, Romansch, Lapps—to be added to the Slavs, Albanians and Germans in Italy.

The East and West differ also in respect of the number and size of states. Whereas the West has eighteen states, the East has only eight, two belonging partly to the West, partly to the East. For the West and East are not divided sharply and by a straight line; Germany and Austria belong both to the West and to the East.

4. Speaking of the East and West of Europe and saying that both halves are not sharply cut, we find a peculiar ethnological zone in what is often called Central Europe. From Trieste—Salonica—Constantinople, up north to Danzig-Petrograd in a line not straight, but curved in the direction of Berlin, in whose neighbourhood live the Slav Sorbs, is a greater number of smaller nations, which were, and still are, under the dominion of Germany, Austria, Turkey and Russia. This zone, composed of East Prussia, Austria-Hungary, the Balkans and the West of Russia, is the real and proper centre of national antagonism. Here the question of nationality and the language question are the political *vis metrix*. It was here that the present war broke out; here is the quarter from which come continual unrest and disturbance for the whole of Europe. This zone is the real kernel of the so-called Eastern Question; this zone supplies the most urgent and clamant cause for remodelling the political organisation of Europe. In this zone the smaller nations are continually striving and fighting for liberty and independence. It is this zone which has confronted the statesmen of Europe with the problem of small nations; and it is the Allies more especially whom this war is forcing to apply themselves to its solution.

The nations of this danger-zone have been free, but have been deprived of their independence; some are highly cultivated and their extent is considerable, they are the greatest among the small nations. Finally, it is necessary to emphasise the striking fact that three of these nations are dismembered in different states; the Serbo-Croats are divided into four states and seven administrative bodies; the Poles into three states; the Czechs and Slovaks into two states; this dismemberment explains the special significance of the Serbo-Croatian, Polish and Bohemian questions.

II

5. We are always speaking of smaller and greater, of small and great nations—what then is the proper definition of a small and of a great nation? What makes a nation great? What is the problem of a small nation, and how does such a problem come to exist?

The very notion of greatness and smallness is relative and correlative; the more so, if the number of the population, or the extent of the territory of a state or a nation, is taken as the principle of the classification.

The most numerous population is in Russia, Germany and Austria-Hungary, and the Russians and Germans are in this sense the greatest nations; the English, French, Italians and Spaniards (we are not considering the nations outside Europe) are smaller. Some sociologists will perhaps put the Russians, Germans and English as one class (eighty-six–forty-five millions), the French, Italians and Spaniards (forty–twenty millions) in a middle class. A third category would be formed by nations under twenty millions, say the Poles, Roumanians, Serbo-Croats and Czechs; then would follow the Portuguese, Swedes, etc., and finally would come what might be described as the fragments or splinters of nations.

I hardly need point out that such a classification is based upon mere numbers and their effects; nor will anyone seek to minimise the decisive material value of these mathematical calculations. We all know *now* what a greater or smaller army means.

But the numerical greatness of a nation is variable and changing. Since the nineteenth century almost all nations have been growing in numbers. All nations, then, are getting larger and statisticians can calculate when the population of the various nations will be doubled. Through this process of growth the numerical relation of the different nations will be changed, owing to the fact that some increase more rapidly than others. The most striking instance, and one which provides a partial explanation of this war, is the slow increase of the population in France compared with its quick growth in Germany. Till 1845 France had a larger population than Germany; indeed, at the end of the eighteenth and at the beginning of the nineteenth century the French were practically the largest nation. A good deal of the French history of that time can be explained by this fact, just as recent German history will become clear if we consider the numerical increase of the population. The Germans themselves boast of this increase as one of their claims to greatness.

We touch here upon the intricate problem of decadence and degeneration; the fact that the annual birth-rate in many countries or parts of countries has been falling in recent years, the fact that changes in the development of the birth-rate are experienced very often and very suddenly, these facts, I say, force every thinking man to abstain from general indictments and condemnations.

The German extreme nationalists have no right to condemn France and other countries in which the increase of the population is slower than in Germany. For not merely is the birth-rate falling in Germany also, but it should be remembered that the overwhelming majority of German economists accept in their theory of population the leading ideas of Malthus and are not inclined to see in this precipitate augmentation of the population an undoubted proof of physical and moral vigour.

But let us assume for the moment that the increase of the population, the surplus of the birth-rate over the death-rate, can be applied as a standard to physical and even moral health and strength. In that case the population principle applies as much to Germany as to other countries. Students of the question know that England during the nineteenth century is the only instance of a country where the population was trebled; and it is equally worth noting that in the Bohemian countries the Czech population increased more rapidly than the German population. Will the German ultra-nationalists admit the consequences of their own logic in these and other cases?

To sum up the argument: Physical greatness and strength, being *ipso facto* always relative and correlative, is no warrant, no foundation of right and of prerogatives; seventy is certainly far more than ten, but have the seventy the right to deprive the ten of their bread? Have they the *right* to use force?

6. The German jingoes appeal to history. History, they argue, shows that small states are slowly but surely disappearing and serving as a material for the big ones. Compare the hundreds of small states in the Middle Ages and even in modern times—they are absorbed and swallowed up by the bigger ones; Prussia herself is an instance of such absorption, but France, Italy, England also; in a word, all big states were formed out of small ones. History, then, proves that the law of political development makes the formation of great states and nations unavoidable. Small nations and states, under the most favourable circumstances, have only a temporary duration: historical development favours and promotes the growth of big nations and states. Germany is big, bigger than the rest, with one exception, which is more apparent than real; therefore her legitimate aim is World-Policy, World-Power!

Let us probe to the bottom this Pan-Germanic imperialist theory. It is quite true that many hundreds of small states—city states—were absorbed by one state growing bigger. But in France, Italy, etc., partly even in Prussia, this process was a gathering of the same people, of the same nation, not a subduing of foreign nations. Though of course Prussia and other states subjugated foreign nations too.

If history proves that small states and nations are ephemeral, it proves the same of big states—remember the Oriental empires, Alexander the Great, the Greeks and Romans, the Franks, the old German Empire, Napoleon. All these states—not nations—were temporary also. The real meaning of these political, un-national formations is misunderstood by the Pan-Germanists, and the arguments upon which they are based are false.

History is a process of integration, but at the same time of disintegration; the double process appears as the strengthening of individualism and the simultaneous growth of collectivism. History tends not towards uniformity, but towards variety, towards organised variety, which very often is misrepresented as barren, monotonous, indiscriminate uniformity.

Speaking politically, the centralising tendencies in social life are steadily counterbalanced by the striving for autonomy and federation in all its variety. Centralised absolutism is everywhere checked by freedom, the centralising tendencies of aristocracy are weakened by the individualistic tendencies of democracy. This double process pervades all departments of social life.

History thus refutes the Pan-German argument. History shows that national states develop in Europe. And History is in favour not only of big, but also of medium-sized and small national states.

History is in favour of all individuals, of individualism in general; nations are natural organisations of homogeneous individuals, and states, being more artificial organisations, are more and more adapted to the nations. So general is this tendency that the numerical strength of the nations does not play a decisive part.

History shows that since the eighteenth century the principle of nationality has grown stronger, and received more and more political recognition. National individualities, their language and culture have steadily gained ground all over Europe, and linguistic rights have been gradually codified. These rights have been, and still are, advocated by Italy, by the Austro-Hungarian and Balkan nations; they are advocated by Germany herself. How then can Germany or any other nation claim for herself this right, and at the same time refuse it to others?

How strong and far-reaching national feeling and ideas have become in modern times, is proved by the revival of oppressed nationalities in all states. The Renaissance of the Bohemian people is a specially striking instance, and a confirmation of the general national principle. The social unit of conscious nations, breaking the old political boundaries, is the real, because the all-comprising, social unit, the old state being the organ of political and military conquest. The function of the state changed, therefore, and changed in accordance with the development of culture. Austria and Prussia are classical instances of the antagonism of state and nationality. The state is autocratic, ruling and domineering, the nation is democratic, administering, social, developing from within. The states therefore are adapted to the nations.

History further shows that the strengthening of national feeling does not prevent the growth of internationalism and internationalisation. I am not playing with words when I draw a sharp distinction between inter-*nationalism* and inter-*statism*. (I hope the philologists will pardon the word.) True nationalism is not opposed to internationalism, but we abhor those nationalist jingoes who in the name of nationalism oppress other nations, and we reject that form of international cosmopolitanism which in fact recognises only one—its own nation—and oppresses the others. True internationalism is not oppression, but neither is it a-nationalism nor anti-nationalism.

We learn from history that the warlike spirit tends to diminish, that militarism is getting more and more defensive after having been offensive; we learn from history that peoples and nations are more and more ready to work for themselves, without depending on the labour of others. Idleness, the oppressive form of aristocracy, whether in individuals, in classes, in nations and in races, is diminishing. History finally shows that brute force and quantity is less and less esteemed. In all nations the best men are agreed in prizing spiritual and moral forces; humanity is the effective watchword of the champions of all nations.

It is true, and history confirms it, that mankind strives for unity, but it does not strive for uniformity. World-federation, not world-power. *Consensus gentium*—not slavery of nations and races; the Organisation—not the Conquest, of Europe.

If I am not mistaken, this war is a revelation of this historic truth. No *Herrenvolk*, but national equality and parity: *Liberté*, *Egalité*, *Fraternité* among nations as among individuals. These political principles, proclaimed in France in the name of humanity, are the foundation of democracy within the single nations, and they are the foundation of democratic relations between states and nations, of democratic internationalism.

The Pan-Germans appeal in vain to history; the facts are against them. History most assuredly is *vitae magister*, the teacher for life; but there is history and history. In fact, history does not prove anything, for all facts are equally historical: history gives us as many examples of brutality as of humanity, of truth as of falsehood. The Huns also are historical. The real question has always been, and will always be, whether we are to bow unquestioningly before all historical facts, or whether we are resolved to master them. I am an adherent of realism; but the spiritual and moral forces in society and their growth are not less real than the Prussian generals; we can and must accept political realism, but we never can approve of the *Realpolitik* of Treitschke, Mommsen, Lagarde, Bernhardi, etc., who have converted anthropology into zoology. I say that, though I am speaking in the country of Darwin and his theory of the survival of the so-called fittest.

III

7. Smaller and small national states could exist very well, in fact, they do exist: out of the twenty-eight states at the very most seven can be classified as great or greater; in other words, the small states outnumber the great by three to one. On a basis of mere size, then, we are not surprised to hear that there is only one great state, only one great nation entitled to world-power.

The conditions of political independence for small states are the same as for the bigger ones. Small and big states have the same natural frontiers: mountain-chains (the Pyrenees—the Bohemian mountains), great rivers, etc. The big, and almost all small, states are on the sea; only Switzerland and Serbia are land-locked, but then it is just Switzerland which provides eloquent proof that a small state can flourish without a coast-line. Many of the smaller nations (Czechs, Magyars, etc.) are without the sea.

On the whole, the so-called national frontiers are political, they were chosen by the states for strategical reasons. The nations spread regardless of natural frontiers; these frontiers are losing more and more their political importance, for culture and the progress of culture means the control and mastery of nature and her blind forces.

States and nations, even when small, have been able to protect their independence: take for instance small Montenegro and the other Balkan nations against Turkey, Holland against Spain, Switzerland (in its smaller size) against Austria, etc. The biggest states have been unable to resist small but determined nations, whose spirit is expressed in the famous words of the Bohemian patriot, Dr Rieger: 'We won't give in!'

The physical, mental and moral qualities of smaller nations are just as good as those of their greater neighbours and oppressors. Are the Serbians less brave than the Austrian-Germans? the Czechs less energetic and strenuous for having conserved and strengthened their nationality against the Germans? Denmark is probably the most cultured country in Europe. Bohemia has fewer illiterates than the Austrian-Germans.

Such instances could easily be multiplied; but I am ready to concede that on the other hand small nations labour under certain disadvantages. A small nation has a more limited number of hands and heads: the division and organisation of labour, physical and mental, is less adequate. There is a smaller number of specialists; wealth and comfort are more restricted. But here, too, there are exceptions: take Holland, Switzerland, Bohemia, etc. Some small nations are apt to acquire a peculiar form of timidity, a lack of daring and enterprise; occasionally even a kind of cringing want of frankness. But are these qualities not due to the effect of prolonged oppression? To be sure, these and other drawbacks, in so far as they exist, exist only under given circumstances, under the pressure of the existing system of rapacious militarism and economic exploitation. Let the smaller nations be free: do not interfere, leave them alone, and these drawbacks will soon disappear.

But small nations have also some advantages over greater nations; both drawbacks and advantages are relative.

A smaller nation develops a certain many-sidedness; every individual force and talent is valued and used: labour and effort, and indeed the whole working system, are intensified. It is a well-known fact that the lands of small farmers produce relatively much more than do large estates. The whole nation is, so to speak, well-kneaded. Palacký, our great Bohemian historian, exhorted his nation to treble and even to increase tenfold its labours; small nations are indeed nations of workers. In a smaller community there is a more intensive inter-communion of men, ideas and feelings; people know each other, they can be more easily united; though of course this intimacy also has its drawbacks. Dr Fisher, the Vice-Chancellor of Sheffield University, in his essay on the value of small states, brings out the fact that democracy, the direct participation of the people in the government, can be better developed in small states. He adduces many instances; and it was certainly this idea that inspired Rousseau's proposal to divide the big state into small communities. Sociologists and historians know that the administrative machinery of the modern state grew out of the small administration of cities. The great cities in big states are a remedy against indefinite expansion. I will not conceal the fact that small nations also can be decoyed by tempting imperialist ideals; notable instances are the Magyars, and perhaps the Bulgarians. The poet Kollár, the great apostle of humanity and national reciprocity, rightly observed that small nations can be very intolerant.

The German Imperialists often tell us that small nations cannot produce great men: great men require, we are told, a great environment, the communion of many and great spirits. I do not believe it, and I take the instance of my own country. The whole world knows and esteems John Hus, the whole world has learnt from the educationalist Comenius; the religious community of the United Brethren is a marvel of history, as historians say; the founder of this church, Peter Chelčický, the great predecessor of Tolstoï, is more and more appreciated. Our nation was the first to break the spiritual centralisation of the Middle Ages, and to dare the Reformation. Žižka, the leader of the Hussites, is the founder of modern strategy.

The bravery and heroism of small nations has been mentioned. Hussite Bohemia faced the whole of Central Europe; historians report that the Germans fled on hearing the Hussite battlesong. (Would that the Allies could compose a similar song!) But whatever shortcomings or even faults small nations may have, they love their country and their people, and this love prompts them to energetic action in the fields of politics and culture.

I speak of culture. That is a difficult and intricate social factor. I will only express my point of view. Culture is not the product of any one nation, big or small: there are various types and different degrees of culture. I am no blind follower of Rousseau or mere admirer of the primitive stages of culture, but it is a very great disability not to accept the various forms and degrees of culture as represented by the many nations and parts of nations, and not to understand that each nation must work out its culture alone and independently, and not simply take that of another nation, even if it be called a higher culture. Passive acceptance of this kind may be convenient, but it is dangerous and detrimental.

Culture cannot be knocked and drubbed into nations. If the Germans speak of their being supporters of civilisation—'Kulturträger'—it is only a pretext. A Polish politician is absolutely right in denouncing forced denationalisation as one of the great social evils.

Dr Fisher, speaking of the rude and valiant Serbian peasant, very aptly alludes to the ballads which sing of the battle of Kosovo, and to their great educational influence on the Southern Slavs. During the last war against the Turks I happened to be in Serbia, and a Serbian officer told me his experience on the battlefield. When at the head of his regiment of peasant soldiers he reached the plain of Kosovo, the famous 'Field of the Blackbirds', a deathlike silence seized the whole detachment; men and officers, without any command, uncovered their heads, crossed themselves, and each of them tried to tread softly, so as not to disturb the eternal sleep of their heroic ancestors. (Here my friend, quite lost in the remembrance of that great experience, unconsciously imitated their gait, and his voice fell to a whisper as he recalled the silence of his soldiers.) Many of the weather-beaten faces were bedewed with unconscious tears, as was my friend's face as he spoke. I, too, was deeply affected by the recital of his experience. How many of the German professors, who to-day are raving against Serbia, do you think are worth one tear of these illiterate peasants?

If time permitted, I might analyse the drawbacks of great nations. Germany herself, who claims to be the greatest of all, is tormented by a perpetual unrest. Greatness imposes a duty—to protect the smaller brothers and at least help them to join and organise their federations. The Balkan peoples tried it, but no help came to them from Europe. In all nations the need of social reform is recognised; the weak are to be protected by the strong and by the state. An analogous principle holds good in the relation of big to small states and nations. As there is no Superman, so there is no Super-right of great nations. The great nation has no right to use its smaller neighbours as the tools of imperialistic fancy, and of an inordinate craving for power. On the other hand, the small nations must not try to imitate the great; they must be satisfied to go their own way.

8. Pleading for the independence of small nations, I am not ignorant of the sophistical objections masquerading as arguments, that the Lapps cannot form a state and the Kalmucks cannot have an university. The question is, whether nations conscious of their nationality, and proving the possibility of political independence by their economic and cultural progress, and by their claims and efforts for liberty, can be independent. Take, for instance, the

Poles, Serbo-Croats and Czechs; these nations are the biggest of the smaller nations (twenty to ten millions) that have been independent: they reached a high degree of culture, they strive, and even fight, for liberty, for they are thoroughly conscious of their nationality and are determined not to abandon their historical and national rights.

It is a matter of course that there are different degrees and forms of independence. Sovereignty is relative, for the economic and cultural interdependency of all nations is growing. Even the greatest states are dependent on other states; the Triple Alliance and Triple Entente are the very proof of it. Europe is getting more and more federalised and organised. And it is in this given situation and development that the small nations reclaim the right of being peaceably inserted in the growing organisation of Europe. The degree and the form of independence (autonomy within a state—federation—suzerainty—personal union, etc.), in every individual case, will easily be found and formulated according to constitutional rules and laws, when once the principle has been acknowledged.

9. Great Britain came into this war to protect little Belgium, and now with her allies she is faced by the task of protecting Serbia. This evolution of the war is almost logical, for Germany's aim is and was Berlin-Bagdad, the employment of the nations of Austria-Hungary as helpless instruments, and the subjection of the smaller nations which form that peculiar zone between the West and the East of Europe. Poland, Bohemia, Serbo-Croatia (the Southern Slavs) are the natural adversaries of Germany, of her *Drang nach Osten*; to liberate and strengthen these smaller nations is the only real check upon Prussia. Free Poland, Bohemia and Serbo-Croatia would be so-called buffer states, their organisation would facilitate and promote the formation of a Magyar state, of Greater Roumania, of Bulgaria, Greece and the rest of the smaller nations. If this horrible war, with its countless victims, has any meaning, it can only be found in the liberation of the small nations who are menaced by Germany's eagerness for con-

quest and her thirst for the dominion of Asia. The Oriental question is to be solved on the Rhine, Moldau and Vistula, not only on the Danube, Vardar or Maritza.

Great Britain protecting the liberty of Belgium was led by the right feeling of justice; all nations, especially the unfree, appreciated her noble decision: the fact that Great Britain, in protecting Belgium, protects herself and Asia, does not impair her merit. Justice is not only noble, it is quite sensible and useful too.

I will conclude with a confession. I prepared this lecture at the very moment when Serbia was about to be attacked by Germany and her baggage-porters Austria-Hungary and Bulgaria. But more than once the sceptical thought has struck me: is this the time for *talking* about small nations, when the vital thing is simply to afford protection to one of them? Feeling this incongruity, I will comfort myself with the saying of a Slav thinker: 'A good word is a deed also.' I can at least promise that all the lecturers at the new School of Slavonic Studies will spare no effort to make it a success and through it to contribute, however imperfectly, to drawing closer the relations between Britain and the Slavonic world.

CHAPTER V

At the Eleventh Hour

A MEMORANDUM ON THE MILITARY SITUATION

(Circulated in April 1916 in London)

FIRST PART. *Military Strength of the Belligerent States*

1. False Reports of the Enemy's Military Weakness. 2. Amount of Population of the Belligerent States. 3. The German Army. 4. The Austro-Hungarian Army. 5. The Turkish and Bulgarian Armies. 6. Grand Total of the Enemy. 7. The Allied Armies. 8. Grand Total of the Allied Armies. 9. Comparison of the Enemy's Forces with those of the Allies. 10. Advantages of the Enemy. 11. German Drawbacks (or apparent Drawbacks). 12. The Austrian Army compared with the German Army. 13. The British Army. 14. The Battle of Ctesiphon—Gallipoli—Help for Serbia. 15. The French Army. 16. Prussian Militarism and the Allies. 17. The Russian Army. 18. Lack of Co-operation and Unity among the Allies. 19. The Navy.

SECOND PART. *What is to be Done?*

20. More Soldiers! 21. Is a Prolonged War advantageous to the Allies? 22. Will Economics end the War? 23. Japan and the War. 24. Necessity of a Political as well as a Strategical Plan. 25. The German Political Programme: Pan-German Central Europe or 'Berlin-Bagdad'. 26. Austria and the Magyars as the tools and puppets of Pan-Germanism. 27. The War in the Balkans: the three Allied Powers—Britain, France, and Russia—must rely on themselves. 28. The political programme of the Allies: Central Europe, not German, but European.—Liberty of all nations, also of small nations. 29. Independent Poland—Independent Bohemia—Independent Greater Serbia. 30. Germany's weak spot is in the East. 31. France and Russia—Britain and Russia. 32. Austria and Germany once more. 33. How Germany's retreat and defeat would take place. 34. The Neutrals and Germany's defeat. 35. The economic significance of Free Central Europe: Boycott of Germany.

PREFACE

This Memorandum was originally intended by its author for the use of his personal friends in this country. But in view of the weightiness of its arguments and the great reputation of its author, we felt very strongly that it ought to be more widely circulated. As there are obvious objections to publication, it was decided to issue it as a confidential memorandum, for distribution among a strictly limited number of persons.

Professor Masaryk ought to-day to need no introduction even to English readers. He is not merely one of the acknowledged leaders of the Bohemian national movement, but was also one of the most marked personalities in the Austrian Parliament before the war drove him into exile. He has been a life-long democrat and enemy of reaction and militarism: his memorable speech on the Agram Treason Trial, and his pitiless exposure of the forgeries of the Friedjung Trial in 1909, created a sensation throughout Europe. He is also one of the leading Slav thinkers of his time, and his book on *Russia and Europe* greatly increased an already great reputation. London University has honoured herself not less than him by appointing him Lecturer in Slav Literature and Sociology at the New School of Slavonic Studies.

Professor Masaryk's knowledge of Austria-Hungary, Germany, Russia, and the Balkans is profound, and his knowledge of France, Italy, and Britain far from negligible. He has been for years a member of the Austrian Parliament, and on several occasions of the Austrian Delegation (which, under the constitution of the Dual Monarchy, exercises joint control with the Hungarian Delegation over the three Joint Ministries of Foreign Affairs, War, and Finance). He has even been a member of the special committee of that Delegation dealing with the Austro-Hungarian Army. He was thus obliged to follow attentively all military questions and to study the whole problem of military administration. He is thus obviously specially qualified to use the comparative method in dealing with the armies of the belligerent countries.

It only remains to be said that in circulating this Memorandum we do so from a general sense of its importance, without necessarily committing ourselves to agreement with it in every detail.

RONALD M. BURROWS
R. W. SETON-WATSON

KING'S COLLEGE, LONDON
7 January 1916

FIRST PART. *MILITARY STRENGTH OF THE BELLIGERENT STATES*

1. False Reports of the Enemy's Military Weakness

The figures of the strength of the various armies and their losses obviously must be ascertained in the first place. The principal question is how many fighting and military forces in general (reserves, provisions, supply department, railway service, etc.) the various States can bring forth, if the war is to last for a considerable space of time.

Just now we often read, even in serious papers, that the Germans fighting in Russia are beginning to be short of men. But this shortage (if it exists) can be only temporary, as the Germans and Austrians can still raise considerable numbers of men, and, indeed, are actually raising them.

Another very frequent statement relates to the quality of the enemy's soldiers. Even authorities like General Galliéni proclaim (*Sunday Times*, 5 December) that the German troops are exhausting themselves, and that the quality of the German soldier is rapidly deteriorating. But in the same paper for 23 November, in an article on the physique of the German troops, it is pointed out that the reports that the enemy has been compelled to fall back on unfit material in recruiting for his armies, are not trustworthy. The article quotes German official sources.

As a rule the figures of the enemy's strength and quality, as given in the papers, are very misleading, because one statement usually contradicts the other. I am surprised that the Censors in England, France and Russia allow such statements to be printed; German papers are evidently not allowed to do so. I have observed that such statements have a bad effect not only on the general public, but also on the officers and the soldiers who read the papers.

It is surely of great importance that the officers should have a correct view of the quantity and quality of the enemy.

2. Amount of Population of the Belligerent States

Since the beginning of the war figures have often been adduced showing the numbers of the whole population of the Allies as well as of the enemy. These figures are, of course, very comforting: the Allies having an overwhelming majority on a basis of population.

Great Britain	47 millions	Germany	68 millions
Colonies	375	Colonies	16
France	40	Austria-Hungary	51
Colonies	54	Turkey	21
Russia	170	Bulgaria	4½
Italy	36		
Belgium	7		
Colonies	20		
Serbia	4½		
Montenegro	½		
Allies	305	Enemy	144½

Even if we do not count the colonies, these figures are very favourable to the Allies, giving them almost [*sic*] twice as much as the enemy.

The same favourable proportion is arrived at by a comparison of the figures showing the percentage of the male population between the ages of 20 and 50 in all the countries concerned. These give the following numbers of men (men, not soldiers):

Great Britain	8.5–9 millions*	Germany	14½ millions
France	8	Austria-Hungary	10
Russia	34	Turkey	4
		Bulgaria	0.9
	51		29†

* For Great Britain the number of men between 18–40 amounts to 8.1 millions.

† These and all other figures given in the Memorandum are rounded off and put only approximately.

This proportion is greatly changed as soon as we compare the figures of the respective armies. Everyone knows that Germany and her tributaries have hitherto succeeded in throwing against the allied armies superior or at least equal forces.

3. The German Army

German official statistics give the following more specific figures:

Landsturmpflichtig (17–45, liable to service in the Landsturm), 20·5 per cent of the male population.

Militärpflichtig (from 20 years, liable to service in the Army), 14 per cent of the male population.

The German Handbook of the Army for 1912 gives the direct numbers of men available for the service:

4,215,000	trained
5,683,000	untrained
9,898,000	

According to reliable information from Germany, the Germans had, up to August–September 1915, mobilised 60 per cent of the men between 19 and 45—i.e. approximately 8,500,000. Of these 3,400,000 are lost (killed, unfit for further service, missing, etc.), leaving 5,100,000 still available. Now they are calling up the men from 45 to 50, as well as the men of the younger classes, who were not taken from among the 40 per cent already mentioned.

Out of this reserve Germany can levy a large number of new soldiers. It will depend upon what percentage is taken. Forty per cent make 5,600,000; the number of men from 45 to 50 gives 2,000,000. Germany therefore still has 7,600,000 men, out of whom she can put at least 2,000,000 more in the field. It is possible that even men over 50 and of 18 would be taken. The number of men required to keep going industry and commerce is now considerably less than before the war, because all industries are on a reduced footing.

The decisive question is what quantity of equipment and armament Germany has. In any case, the strength of the German Army must not be underestimated, for the German war industry is strong and effective.

4. The Austro-Hungarian Army

Austria-Hungary has up till now mobilised about 4,000,000, and of these at best 2,000,000 are still fit for service. (The Austrian losses are known to include 930,000 prisoners in Russia, 70,000 prisoners in Serbia, 537,000 killed, 90,000 permanently disabled.) Over 1,250,000 are probably now at the front.

But Austria-Hungary is now calling up the classes from 18 to 50, and that would give an additional 4,000,000. The first mobilisation was not strictly carried out; but now all classes are closely examined, and a much higher percentage is taken—on an average 70 per cent, and in the Slav districts of Austria-Hungary as much as 90 per cent. The new levies consist of the following classes:

(1) Men of 24–37, second revision, May–June.
(2) Men of 18, June.
(3) Men of 43–50, July–September.
(4) Men born in the years 1891, 1895, 1896, October.
(5) Men of 37–42, second revision, November–December.
(6) Third revision of all men of 18–50, January–February, 1916.

This gives the high total of 4,000,000. Of these at least 250,000 will be dismissed as unfit, and of the remaining 3,750,000 at least 2,250,000 can be sent to the front, while the rest accounts for the reserves and the service behind the front. That would give about 3,500,000 combatants.

For more detailed figures see *La Nation Tchèque*, 15 October, 1915.

5. The Turkish and Bulgarian Armies

The Turkish Army may amount to 1,000,000 (rather less!), while the Bulgarians can put about 300,000 men actually into the field.

6. Grand Total of the Enemy

	TOTAL EFFECTIVES		AT THE FRONT	
	At present	Next Spring	At present	Next Spring
Germany	5,500,000	8,100,000	4,500,000	5,500,000
Austria-Hungary	2,000,000	5,750,000	1,500,000	3,500,000
Turkey	1,000,000	1,000,000	1,000,000	1,000,000
Bulgaria	300,000	300,000	300,000	300,000
	8,800,000	15,150,000	7,300,000	10,300,000

Once more it must be emphasised that the real number of fighting men will depend on the quantity of uniforms, rifles, ammunition, etc., and, of course, the same holds good with the Allies.

7. The Allied Armies

The Russian Army official reports gave the total of trained men as 7,668,000. Of these 7,000,000 may have been mobilised; but by now almost 4,000,000 of that can be eliminated as killed, unfit, missing, etc. With some new additions the Russian Army may be estimated at 3,500,000.

The French Army. The Deputy Bérenger, member of the Senatorial Army Committee, gives, on 22 September, the total of the French Army as 5,000,000, of which 3,000,000 would be at the front.

The British Army. According to the declaration of Mr Asquith in the House of Commons on 21 September Great Britain has levied an army of 3,000,000, in which the Navy and the Colonials are not included.

The Serbian and Italian Armies. The Serbians, on the eve of the recent invasion, had about 300,000 men. Italy could have a considerable army; she was expected to mobilise at least 1,200,000 men.

8. Grand Total of the Allied Armies

	Total at present	At the Front at present
Russia	3,500,000	3,000,000
France	5,000,000	3,000,000
Great Britain	3,000,000	1,000,000*
Serbia	300,000	160,000
Italy	800,000	600,000
Belgium	100,000	100,000
	12,700,000	7,860,000

* Mr Asquith, on 21 December, stated in the House of Commons that there are one and a quarter million men fighting in the various theatres of war.

9. Comparison of the Enemy's Forces with those of the Allies

At present the Allies have larger armies, and they even outnumber the Enemy at the front; but next spring the Enemy will be much stronger than he is now, as he is levying great forces. The Allies, of course, are doing the same, and so it will depend not so much upon which side will have more men next Spring, as upon which will have the larger number of properly equipped soldiers.

10. Advantages of the Enemy

At present the Allies outnumber the Enemy; they have more men, perhaps even more soldiers. Why, then, is the Enemy more victorious? Only one answer is possible. The Enemy uses his forces better and more effectively than the Allies.

(1) The Enemy was better prepared for the war. Indeed, it is not too much to say that only he was prepared. Even France, in spite of 1870–71, in spite of ideas of revenge, was not prepared. Russia may be said to have been better prepared than might have

been expected, while Britain, with the exception of the Navy, was not prepared at all.

The Austrian Army was not well prepared, as was proved by the defeats which she suffered in the first phase of the war.

(2) The decisive result of being prepared was that Germany started with greater forces than the Allies, at least in the West. It was only in the course of the war that the Allies could equal, and later on outnumber, the Enemy.

(3) The Enemy, as his countries are in close neighbourhood, was able to centralise his forces. At the beginning of the war Austria proceeded more independently, but her failures induced her to accept the German leadership. At present Berlin is the head, the only deciding head, of the Enemy, while the Allies are divided into four headquarters. In war a single narrow-minded leader is better than ten leaders of genius who are not united.

(4) This centralisation and unity is not only strategical; industry, commerce, and railways are centralised and unified as well, and therefore more effective.

(5) The Enemy from the beginning had a clearer political plan of what he wanted to achieve.

The Germans have a very large political literature, in which the Pan-German plan was discussed and, in the course of the discussion, clearly shaped. It is a mistake to believe that Pan-Germanism was, and is, merely Utopian. There was, and is, a Utopian element in it, but on the whole it very soon developed into a realistic doctrine, culminating in the plan of uniting all Germans in an economic organisation of the whole of Central Europe. (A more detailed exposition of Germany's political plan in this war will be given later, § 25.)

Until now the Allies have had no such plan.

A political plan is essential for an army. In the German Army there are thousands and thousands of officers of all ranks who prosecute the Pan-German idea, and not only officers, but hundreds and thousands of soldiers as well, have been educated in Pan-German ideas.

The leaders of an army must have a positive political plan, so as to know what territory to occupy, how to behave in the occupied territory, what to do there, and how to prepare for the future, etc.

(6) Public opinion, especially in Germany, is well led by the Universities and the whole machinery of schools, journalism and war literature. The Germans made a very effective use of Science. Germany has an effective journalistic service in neutral countries. The Germans have a more effective and much more extensive agitation abroad.

(7) The Germans are strong by their *pénétration pacifique*, not only in the neutral countries (the United States and America in general, Switzerland, Holland, etc.), but even in the belligerent countries themselves the Germans even to-day exert a very appreciable influence, sometimes amounting to pressure.

(8) The Germans have made a good strategical use of the railways. They sent their troops by fast trains from West to East or vice versa. That enabled them to have their soldiers in masses, though inferior in numbers. Russia, as well as Austria, and apparently the French and English also, transport their soldiers in very slow trains.

(9) Germans have made a good strategical use of automobiles (e.g. capture of Liége).

(10) The Germans made use of heavy guns at a very early stage, if not from the very beginning, especially for destroying the trenches.

(11) The Germans have a great number of mitrailleuses. As one mitrailleuse equals in its shooting power fifty foot-soldiers, the great number of mitrailleuses serves as a substitute for soldiers.

From German sources it has been reported that they have 40,000 mitrailleuses, and it is said that they use them more especially against the British troops.

I rather expected that the Allies would invent some new system of rifles or guns to make up for their shortcomings. I expected some decisive invention in the flying department (especially the regulation of aiming from airships). To my regret I learn that the Germans have invented new automatic rifles, firing 25 shots a minute.

(12) In this connection the German submarines may be mentioned. On the Continent they made a great impression not only on the civilian public; the Germans appeared as inventors and innovators even in naval strategy. The British public, of course, knows more about the real situation.

(13) The Germans derived from their offensive and offensivity all the benefit usually ascribed to these tactics; the Allies proceeded more passively, allowing themselves to be moved by the governing will of the advancing enemy.

(14) The Germans have so far displayed a great assurance of final victory; neither the army nor the general public were weakened by doubts and disquieting reflections. Only in the latest phase some scepticism is arising, but so far it is not victory that is in doubt; it is only the attainment of the full aim, as proposed at the beginning of the war, that is questioned.

II. German Drawbacks (or apparent Drawbacks)

The German strategists do not in any way strike me as men of genius. But they are conscientious, energetic, well-trained generals. The glorification of Hindenburg was facilitated by the treachery of Myasoyedov. But that's just it—Germany has no such traitors in high places!

The German officer is a good soldier, and the men are very good and well trained. For instance, Germany spent a relatively much higher proportion of her War Budget upon rifle practice than other countries did. On the whole, Germany's secret is assiduous thinking, the employment of Science and its practical consequences, being prepared and looking ahead; above all, enforcing the co-ordination, organisation, and centralisation of all their forces.

But the German system is not without its shortcomings.

(1) The continuous offensive involves a danger of exhaustion, especially for the Army. Germany sent all her best troops to the front at the very beginning; the sharp offensive brought them considerable losses, as great masses were engaged.

No doubt the new reinforcements will be weaker, but not so weak, I think, as is often stated in the Press.

To be able to take the offensive, the Germans have a relatively weaker reserve of men. The new levy must create a reserve and this reserve will be formed of older men, but perhaps the Allies will also be forced to levy older men.

> Compare the following: *Westminster Gazette*, 20 October: 'I learn from a reliable source (says the Central News Amsterdam correspondent to-day) that within a short time men between the ages of fifty and fifty-five, who have already served in the army, will be called up in Germany.' *Standard*, Amsterdam, 10 November: 'On November 15th Landsturm between the ages of forty and forty-three, who have not yet served, will be called up at Aix-la-Chapelle.' *Times*, 3 December: 'A Bill has been introduced in the Hungarian Parliament making men of fifty to fifty-five years of age liable to military service, but only to be employed within the country.' *Times* and other papers reported, 13 December, that Austria is going to levy even boys of seventeen years (?).

(2) Though German industry has been reduced, and consequently a considerable number of young workmen were set free for the war, yet the Germans need a great mass of strong and healthy people to keep their best industries going. That is the drawback of the industrialisation of the war.

This explains why Austria-Hungary, having a smaller industry, is able to raise a relatively larger army. Austria-Hungary did not call up all her forces at the beginning, as the Germans did, and therefore to-day she may still have relatively greater numbers of new soldiers.

(3) The dashing offensive against Paris, and then against Russia, did not succeed fully. The German soldiers and the public are beginning to feel uneasy.

(4) I am inclined to think that the strategical plan of Germany miscarried from the beginning. Germany overrated her ally Austria, and she underrated Russia. Leaving the Russians and Serbians to Austria, the Germans made their perfidious invasion of Belgium and threw themselves against Paris, but being obliged to retreat in France they invaded Russia and Serbia. It would have served the German plan much better not to have violated Belgium, but to have defended their relatively short frontier against France and to have attacked with all violence the Russian Army. This was all the more to be expected, because Germany, led by the Emperor himself, in the beginning of the war proclaimed Russia as the deadly enemy. It is quite evident that the Germans changed their original plan, doing, after a year's experience, what they might have done at the beginning.

(5) Very much is written about the starvation in Germany, and about the need of cutting off the supplies of the necessary food, wool, metals, etc.

I fear many futile hopes are still cherished in that respect. Food in Germany is scanty, but the people are not starving. Frugality and temperance, even fasting from time to time, does not demoralise a people; on the contrary, it may stimulate and make them more energetic. Soldiers who eat too much, fat soldiers, are worse than hungry ones—that is an old experience, of which we may read in Caesar's Commentaries.

Whether Germany is short of cotton, metals, etc., is a question of fact. But there is a good deal of evidence that the neutrals provided Germany with necessaries. For instance, on a single day of last summer Germany got 100 wagons of copper through Switzerland, and to this even French agents are said to have contributed. Now they will have the copper mines in Serbia. The Germans make full use of the industrial establishments of the occupied territories in Belgium, France, Poland: they use the coal mines of France, etc.

(6) The question of the blockade and suppressing German maritime commerce and navigation is too complicated to be discussed here fully; there are English industrial and commercial authorities who do not believe that Germany has been effectively blockaded. The trade of her neutral neighbours with the United States has gone up too much for it to be credible that the Germans did not get the greater part of this trade (in some instances a rise of over 300 per cent above pre-war figures).

The Germans will perhaps lose many business connections, their commerce will be damaged; but on the other hand, they are forced to show restraint, to give up all luxuries and a good deal of comfort. Meanwhile, the logic of the public does not seek the cause of this enforced economy and parsimony in their Government and the Emperor, but in their enemies, especially the English.

To some extent the present economic situation in Germany is the anticipation of the future, when nations, at least the big nations, will be self-sufficing and independent of import or export. At any rate the British Blockade does not hurt Germany's strategical position, at least not for the last period of the war—though perhaps its effects may be more serious in the future.

(7) A word must be said about the climate and nature of Russia. The papers are full of expectations that Winter will be an ally of the Russians. Even some Russian papers write the same. That is a mistake. Cold in winter is not nearly as bad as moisture and rain—the frozen ground actually facilitates communications which are greatly impeded by rains. General Russky declared in an interview very rightly, that 'Winter would seriously modify the war conditions, because the rivers, lakes and marshes being frozen, the defensive will become more difficult, while the offensive will require more numerous effectives'. I had reliable news from Germany, last summer, that the Germans were preparing fur coats and making provisions for the winter campaign.

Nor should it be forgotten that the winter campaign tells very badly on some of the allied troops.

12. The Austrian Army compared with the German Army

The Austro-Hungarian Army is not as good and effective as the German Army.

(1) Austria before and since the annexation of Bosnia-Herzegovina prepared for war, and even mobilised (1908–9, 1912–13), yet her army was not prepared when the war broke out though the tension between her and Russia necessitated careful preparation. Officially the Government and the military authorities proclaimed more than once, that the Austrian Army alone was able to face the Russians and beat them into the bargain. It soon became manifest that the Army was very deficient; the leading was bad, and the commissariat was specially defective; the sanitary department was wretched (scanty equipment of the field hospitals, lack of surgical instruments, X-ray apparatus, etc.).

Even the armament of the troops was inadequate, no provision having been made for the use of heavy guns, and the artillery on the whole was weak. The Russians had an overwhelming artillery, and that was the amazing surprise, for both in Austria and in Germany the Russian Army was looked upon as of no strategical value.

(2) Austria was defeated by the Russians, and by the Serbians. But the defeat restored Austria to life, the danger augmented her forces. And then Germany came to Austria's aid—the Austrian Army was, and is now, directed by the Germans. The German system has been imposed upon its administration, and experience shows that it is effective and works well. We have here a very instructive instance not only of Germany's efficiency, but also of the fact that in war, leadership and the chief command is the deciding factor. If an army of good soldiers fails, it is from the head that the fish stinks (to quote a drastic German proverb). The

war has proved that the soldiers of all the belligerent countries are excellent, each nation having some individual, specific qualities.

The German leading of the Austrian Army paralyses the pro-Allies sympathies of a considerable part of the Austro-Hungarian Army. The war against Serbia and Russia was very popular with the Germans and Magyars; of the other nations the Poles and Ruthenes (excepting the Russophile minority) were warlike in feeling, while the remaining nations were against the war. Of these the Bohemian regiments in particular showed their Slavophil sympathies without reserve, as is generally known; nor did the Serbo-Croats, the Roumanians and Italians like fighting for Austria. Later on, when Italy went against Austria, the Slav troops were sent against Italy, whose claims on Dalmatia wounded the national feelings of the Serbo-Croats, Slovenes and Czechs.

(3) There is one difference between Austria and Germany, which, although already mentioned, I wish to repeat and emphasise: In the first phase of the war Austria did not send to the front so many troops as Germany and, therefore, Austria now has relatively greater reserves of men. Furthermore, Austria's industry needs less men, and this again will allow her to put comparatively more men into the Army. The men have already been called out.

13. The British Army

I am writing these lines in a critical moment: Parliament and the Press are getting more and more restless, the policy of the Government, the Army and its leading is being criticised on all sides. I follow very closely all public utterances and try to learn what sensible people of all classes think, and say. The war lasts long, and the Allies now after the retreat of the Russians are not gaining ground (since the battle of the Marne, that is to say, for over a year!) and as it is generally known—and just this point is emphasised, not only by the official press in Russia, France and England—that the Allies dispose of a greater amount of troops, the disquieting question arises, what is the cause of the deadlock and of the reverses, if the shortcomings in the supply of ammunition have really been removed? I am anxious to discriminate between inconsiderate and unfounded criticism and a conscientious if reluctant expression of 'holy dissatisfaction', as this state of mind under analogous circumstances has been called. The situation is very serious indeed, it cannot be more serious.

I will try to do full justice to the Allies, I will not allow myself to be carried away by the feeling of dissatisfaction, which close observation evokes.

Britain never having been a military state, had no big Army, or rather, British militarism displayed itself in the Navy. From some official hints it is manifest, that Britain joined the Allies on the understanding that she would send only a small army, but would make full use of her Navy and help financially. Unquestionably the British Navy deserves full praise; equal praise must be bestowed upon the financial help, given not only by the State, but by private relief work as well.

Britain having levied 3,000,000 men, did much more than she was expected to do, at any rate more than she was obliged to do. But the development of the war and especially Germany's designs against the British Empire, forced England to protect herself against this unexpected thrust, and, therefore, she has to raise a very large army. I am convinced that the Germans will only be thrown back in the West and defeated, if Britain can bring to the front much more than a million soldiers, perhaps twice that number.

France appears to have called up all the men she had; therefore, Britain and Russia must open their 'reservoirs' of men, if the Germans and their Allies are to be met with an outnumbering army.

Britain should introduce universal compulsory service. This system is more just and democratic, and it is much cheaper.

The British Army must be superior in numbers, because, compared with the German Army, it has some drawbacks due to natural circumstances.

In recent times its only experience of war has been against uncivilised tribes and nations: whereas the Germans have quite a different experience, besides being a military nation *par excellence*. The English resemble in that respect the Russians; although both had one analogous war experience—the Wars with the Boers and Japanese.

The British Army, being raised from non-soldiers, has one great drawback—it has few officers of experience, especially in the higher ranks. That is a very real drawback, which must be taken into consideration; the more so, that the number of previously trained men is also small. Generals cannot be trained in a few months—therefore the most conscientious selection of the best men is necessary.

The papers announced that the British troops are to be drilled for six months; perhaps that is a good and expedient measure for England. In Austria and Germany the drill of the new men lasts only six weeks. It has been tried in Austria to send to the fighting line men after only a four weeks drill, but the experiment failed.

The long drilling period of the English recruits is, I presume, partly due to the voluntary system, getting men little by little; compulsory universal service would shorten the period of drilling.

The British officers look very unmilitary and unwarlike; an eye accustomed to see German, Austrian, and Russian officers, detects at the first glance that the majority are more sportsmen than soldiers. Sport is a good preparatory school to military service, but it is not military service itself. The outfit of an officer is too luxurious and too costly to be military. I do not doubt, of course, that these men will fight very gallantly, that they will die with the greatest dignity, but England does not so much need officers who can die, as officers who can fight and win.

Of course the whole so-called voluntary system with its high pay is unmilitary, at least unwarlike. I read in serious papers, that industry and food production requires so many men, that universal service is impossible. This is a mistake. Universal service would not withdraw the necessary men from industry; it is merely a matter of ascertaining how many men industry requires, and these would then be provided. The Government must, of course, be in a position to know the requirements. Germany has an effective industry in spite of the compulsory system. Britain, of course, cannot compete with Germany (45 millions to 68 millions), but there is Canada, Australia—always assuming that the Navy is able to provide the necessary transport.

One fact has repeatedly forced itself upon my notice here. I find a striking lack of imagination among the English; often even men who are interested in the war as specialists are unable to anticipate the future developments of the situation; there is a peculiar lack of creative imagination in anticipating and foreshadowing the different possibilities. At the same time people are fantastic, constructing rather wild pictures of the nearest future, pictures which are of course merely the fond offspring of their own wishes.

My explanation of the fact is this: The English feel great security on their island; for generations they have felt the satisfaction of being the rulers of the greatest Empire in the world, and they learn from history that they repulsed the attack of Napoleon. It is from this cause that the British have been relatively slow to realise the peculiar importance of the war for their own country. Lulled in security, they still do not realise sufficiently the danger of the near future. The belief in the British Navy and in the protection afforded by the insular position of the country prevents people from seeing the consequences of a German victory. Germany organising Central Europe and utilising it according to the Pan-German programme, would attack England in Asia and Africa. Germany would be richer and would therefore be able to build a great Navy. By and by the insular position of England would become full of danger and isolation. Germany would control Asia and Africa by land, not only from Trieste, etc.

And there is another feature of England in connection with that feeling of security. England is rich, richer than Germany; the

Englishman is accustomed to have his bread and butter, his comforts: a great portion of the nation live even in luxury—the hungry German (even if satiated, the German is in fear of starvation) is always on the *qui vive*, he is more versatile, more imaginative and effective. Again I must lay stress upon the difference between temporary hunger and degrading starvation.

'Business as usual' is a two-edged motto—a watchword and a boast. The English admit quite frankly that they were not prepared for the war, but in doing so they are usually thinking only of military preparation: whereas this unpreparedness is of a wider range and significance. Indeed it will, I believe, be admitted that, so far, Britain has had to pay the premium of apprenticeship. Other nations, especially the Russians (but the Germans also), have also had to learn from experience in this war; but the English have to learn more and they must become quicker in putting the teachings of the war into practice.

14. THE BATTLE OF CTESIPHON—GALLIPOLI—HELP FOR SERBIA

Let me give some concrete instances of this striking deficiency. Take first the battle of Ctesiphon.

As soon as it became manifest that the Germans were approaching Constantinople, it was of vital interest for England to counterbalance the German victory in the Balkans by the possession of Bagdad, the more so as the Germans have been proclaiming for years and years that Constantinople will bring them to Bagdad. But what happened in Mesopotamia? After the first advance towards Bagdad the British troops had to retire, for lack of water. Is it possible in those regions to advance without good supplies of water for men and animals? Was the nature of the territory not known to the British? Did they not learn from the Italians in Tripoli the need of providing water? What kind of intelligence service has the Army in Mesopotamia?

Next day the retirement of the British was explained by the fact that the Turks had much larger forces. But how could it happen that the British did not know at least the approximate strength of the enemy? There were also some rumours that the Arab tribes were treacherous; supposing that this were true, would that be an excuse? The British had been in Mesopotamia long enough for the staff to know the situation.

But the most striking explanation of the Mesopotamian failure was given by Lord Crewe in the House of Lords (7 December). Lord Crewe made two statements: first, that General Townshend had a larger army than his own division; and, secondly, that he had not engaged in the battle on his own personal decision; on the contrary, the competent authorities considered his army sufficient in numbers for the purpose. Lord Crewe explained, with great emphasis, that the advance on Bagdad was contemplated some months ago; that this advance had a political meaning, and that by universal competent military opinion General Townshend's forces were considered to be sufficient. 'The task, however,' he says, 'proved to be a heavier one than was anticipated, owing to the greatly superior forces of the enemy and their powerful armament of artillery.'

Now I admit that a disaster of this kind may happen to any army, but not at such a time and under political and strategical circumstances of such a kind as to demand the utmost effort not only on the part of the staff, but of every single general and officer! A disaster at such a moment as this shows that there must be grave shortcomings in the leading and administration of the army.

The Gallipoli undertaking, the diplomatic and strategical failure to be prepared to help Serbia in time, the fact that German East Africa is to-day still in the hands of the Germans—all these are further indications of the same fact.

The narrowness of the Dardanelles and of the Gallipoli Peninsula should have prevented an attack against Turkey from this side. Both the Straits and the Peninsula can be easily defended by a comparatively small army, without the attacking army being able to make any display of forces.

So far as Serbia is concerned, it was the positive duty of the Allies, and especially of Britain, to come to her aid. But in doing so they were also, it must be remembered, protecting themselves. Britain, being at war with Turkey, had to attack as effectively as possible; that was and is necessary if only for the sake of British prestige in Asia and the Balkans. The attack on Gallipoli and the Dardanelles shows that the obligation of assuming the offensive was felt; but in my opinion the true offensive would have been against Bagdad, with a view to joining hands with the Russians further north, and so eventually threatening Constantinople. In that case the attack on the Dardanelles and Gallipoli would look differently.

How the southern point of Gallipoli and Salonica are to be held can be answered only by strategists, who know the strength of the army at their disposal. The situation is worse now that Bulgarian territory can be used by Turks and Germans. The Turks, Bulgarians and Germans with the Austrians may have 400 + 300 + 200 = 900,000 men: Serbia at the best 160,000—how many have the Allies? Will British troops come via Italy to Albania? Will the Italians take their part and the Russians or the Roumanians? The German leaders will no doubt fortify the whole Greek frontier, if they decide to respect Greece and her peculiar neutrality; but it is probable that they will attack both Salonica and Gallipoli. And Egypt and Bagdad! The political and economic significance of Egypt for Britain has been duly discussed by Pan-German politicians and strategists, and it must be expected that the Germans will not suddenly forget it, now that they are at Constantinople. Again and again one demand must be made: more soldiers, swift decisions and rapid movements! The Germans will do all in their power to weaken Britain and to injure her prestige in the Orient, and I expect a fierce attack on the British troops in the West also.

15. The French Army

Of France I will say little. The views which I have held for many years past on France's role in the future war coincide almost completely with those contained in Colonel Grouard's well-known book (*France et Allemagne—La Guerre éventuelle*). For instance, I never could understand why France built so many fortresses on the frontier; I was of opinion that France should not begin with an offensive, and I was afraid that she was not adequately prepared, whether from the military or the administrative point of view—this and other views I have expressed often before the war, and in a series of articles at the outbreak of the war. In these views I was confirmed by Colonel Grouard; I select his book out of the interesting French military literature, because it is well worth reading even to-day.

To me it was a problem why France, having had the experience of 1870–71 and dreaming of revenge, was not better prepared for the war, though, of course, I could observe that official France during the last few decades had given up the idea of such a revenge and of war in general. As a matter of fact the French Government was taken unprepared, just as England and all the other Allies.

All the more credit is due to France that, though at first she had a smaller army than the Germans, she could put up such resistance and could even gain the battle of the Marne—with the help of British troops. Now she has brought together a very big army, and the spirit of this army is excellent, as is shown by all the reports from the battlefield. I myself was pleasantly surprised during my stay in France by the sober, determined, and unpretentious behaviour of the French officers. The observer is struck by the apparent intelligence of both officers and soldiers. I must say that my French experiences were the most comforting which I have had during the later period of the war. I cannot refrain from praising the determined spirit which pervades the whole French nation. If there was in the first period of the war some indecision even in the Army, there is no longer any trace of it now. The French are more and more conscious of the great importance of the war and of its noble aims. M. Briand's latest utterance is an expression of the general feeling and conviction in France.

16. Prussian Militarism and the Allies

I am not surprised that France and Britain awoke comparatively late to the full consciousness of what this awful war means. France and Britain are parliamentary States. Democracy, though imperfect, is deeply rooted: the struggle for individual freedom is a national ideal: France is a republic. In order that democracy and liberty should be strengthened, the spirit of aristocratism which has hitherto stood for militarism had to be weakened. Hence France and Britain, aiming at democracy, naturally had to suppress or at least mitigate the military spirit. The course which this historical process is taking cannot be discussed here; but it is of great importance to be aware of the fact, to be able to understand the difference between military Germany and democratic France and Britain. I am inclined to believe that all the military and administrative drawbacks and shortcomings of France and Britain are precious proofs of the necessary weakening of militarism. I do not, of course, suggest that all these deficiencies are to be accounted for by real democratism, but a good many of them undoubtedly are.

What holds good of France and England can be to some extent applied to Russia as well, and also to Italy.

But the Allies decided to protect themselves and the small nations; they decided to crush Prussian militarism, and to free Europe from its weight. Militarism no doubt can be weakened by peaceful means, but its attack cannot be repulsed by these means; and it may be argued that the policy of France and Britain was not always consistently democratic, or framed so as to prevent this war and to force Germany morally to a peaceful policy too.

Europe is in a state of transition, and that often means 'halfness'. In any case, once the Allies decided to face Germany on the battlefield, it was necessary for them to know the Germans and their methods, to understand German militarism, and to face it by adequate measures. Once they decided to cast out the devil by Beelzebub, they had to play the devil with the Prussian devil. And the devil is black—you can fight him with pure white, but never with some shade of dingy grey or red, and least of all with a motley display of iridescent hues and colours...

It is only natural that there was a certain amount of practical anti-militarism in some of the armies. But after seventeen months of fighting, not only the Government and the general staff, but every single man must be determined to win the great fight. One can understand Hervé's position before the war, but to-day Hervé himself has taken the only possible and right path—to resist and to win. Liberty and democracy can only be protected and strengthened by determination, heroism, devotion and sacrifice.

Democracy with its Parliamentarism means Parley, means Compromise and the Direct Control of the People, whereas in war, in military and strategic matters, there is no time and no place for any kind of democratic referendum. Time and swiftness of decision means victory.

17. The Russian Army

I happened to be in Berlin several times during the first four months of the war; I heard there many expressions of amazement at the surprising achievements of the Russians. As I have already pointed out, the Germans, partly influenced by the Austrians, underestimated the Russian troops. In point of fact they were much better prepared than the Austrians—they had an overwhelming artillery, the equipment was good, as I heard from many competent quarters in the Austrian Army; and very much praised was the Russian sanitary department.

The invasion of Bukovina and Galicia, the repulse of Hindenburg before Warsaw, etc., were splendid achievements; the victory in Galicia seemed to secure the road for the advance against Berlin, the image of the crushing steam roller became a necessary ingredient and topic of the daily stock of war-illustrations and forecasts. It is only just to say that this premature and hasty idea did not come from Russia only.

The Press of the Allies wrote very uncritically of the greatness and of the masses of Russia, indulging in the false opinion that Russian resources of men are inexhaustible. But 'men' and 'soldiers' are not the same thing. Russia had not the necessary millions of rifles and uniforms, she had not the necessary ammunition, and her quite respectable store of guns was exhausted. And, of course, the very greatness of Russia is her chief strategical source of weakness—the lack of railways and roads.

The Russians, like the British, gathered their military experience from fighting non-European armies; after the war with Japan the whole army and navy were in a state of transformation. It does Russia credit that the expectations of her enemies were deceived. I do not underrate the defeat which followed; and I would not seek to minimise the great masses of captured men and officers; but I cannot abstain from praising the Russian soldier, whose enforced retreat did not bring demoralisation with it. After all, the present defeat is balanced by the previous victory, and a new era is opening for the Russian Army.

If I wrote this Memorandum for Russians, I should have much more to say on the Russian Army and Russian policy; here I content myself with the bare statement, that the Russian defeat was not caused merely by lack of ammunition. We know now, that even the Germans on some occasions were short of ammunition, as they are ready enough to confess to-day. The great shortcoming of the Russian Army was caused by certain peculiar features of the general staff and its relation to the generalissimo; besides there were serious faults in the military administration, and Russian policy in the occupied territories was not worthy of the occasion. The disgraceful affair of Myasoyedov has already been mentioned.

I regretted from the beginning that the Russian campaign did not disclose any real political plan; the liberation of the Poles and other Slavs, the protection of Serbia was proclaimed; but these great aims were not matched by deeds. Very soon it became obvious that Russia's whole policy was dwindling to the annexation of Eastern Galicia; the Balkans, Constantinople and Asia were forgotten, the Army of the Caucasus was doomed to secondary and purely local strategy. Now we see the fruit of the Russian defeat. The Germans are not far from Constantinople, Persia is very disturbed and China may soon follow.

It was in the year 1887 that I learned from a Russian officer, during a visit in Russia, that in case of war with Germany the Germans would try to invade Petrograd, and since that time I had this possibility before my mind, and in an article written at the very beginning of the war expressed the apprehension that the Germans would aim at Petrograd. It is always dangerous to let the enemy create a precedent. Of course the Russians have the precedent of East Galicia and its benefit, but that is of a much lesser value than the German precedent.

The expulsion of the Germans from Russian Poland will be a serious task; the Germans will be very strongly entrenched; the Austrians have fortified, under German leading, all the Carpathian mountain-passes and defiles, and have prepared trenches, the destruction of which will require many batteries of heavy guns. The lessons of the retreat and of the first occupation will, I hope, prevent the reiteration of the bad mistakes made in the administration of the occupied territories, not only towards the Poles and Jews, but also towards the Ruthenes. I am sorry to be obliged to say that the Russians alienated many sympathies there; and it was only the blunders of the Austrian administration after the re-occupation that counter-balanced this loss.

18. Lack of Co-operation and Unity among the Allies

The Allies, then, not being military nations such as the Germans and, therefore, not being as prepared for war as these specialists in soldiering, had to learn by the war. But it is to be hoped that the time of apprenticeship has been served—though, of course, the Germans have learned as well. In any case, in all the countries of the Allies, in Britain just as in France and Russia, the Parliaments and the public expect a more prosperous campaign of their armies. To that end, criticism is becoming general and advice is being given both with regard to the Government and the armies. The changes in the various Governments show that the latter themselves acknowledge that these criticisms are not unfounded or inopportune.

The Times war correspondent (12 November) gives the view of the Russian main headquarters to the effect, that had there been from the beginning of the war a closer co-ordination of the allied armies, we should not have had to deplore the Carpathian adventure, and the temporary eclipse of Russia's military power. I agree with the correspondent; but all the Allies, especially the three Great Powers, are equally responsible for this lack of unity. Moreover the Russian main headquarters obviously should not have executed a strategical plan, the realisation of which depended upon the unity of the Allies, if this unity did not exist.

The universal demand for unity and co-operation is quite just, and, as we see, the military authorities concur with the civilian critics on that point. But if a common plan is demanded, one assumption is tacitly implied, namely, that those whose task it is to co-operate and to devise a plan shall be the right men for the task. Incapable men meeting together in committee will not thereby become capable and efficient. *Capable* men are wanted—whether in the Government, diplomacy, or the armies.

All such questions (for instance the question whether the

Government is to be composed of many or a few members, etc.) are very important, but none the less matters of form. The war is an event so gigantic, that everywhere great men are longed for —men equal to the grandeur of the emergency. The war has made it manifest that, in all countries, many members of the Government, though possibly quite good in times of peace, are not in any way equal to so tremendous an occasion.

The public, therefore, is not content with formal, and proceeds to material, criticism. 'The diplomatists are to blame for our want of success.' 'There have been too many diplomatists and strategists.' 'The military authorities refuse to carry out what the civil authorities propose and demand.' These and kindred objections can be read now every day.

My own experience with Austrian diplomacy makes me prone to join the chorus of those who criticise diplomatists; but it is not they only who have been to blame. I do not defend them, because I know quite well what some diplomatists of the Allies have done in the various countries; many people know it and point their fingers at several personages. Possibly some of them could defend themselves by arguing that their Government very often did not listen to their reports; but in any case it is the various Governments and Foreign Offices which are responsible for their diplomacy.

I would insert here a word on the military attachés. All the Governments have had their military attachés in Berlin for years past. What were these gentlemen doing in Berlin? What did they see and hear there and at the many manœuvres? But I will be just—the German attachés were no better! They did not see that Russia was more prepared than was expected: they did not see that Austria was much less prepared than she herself pretended: they did not see the excellent ·75 mm. guns of the French.

After the war objections of this kind may serve for reconstructing the whole administrative machinery of the State; but the results of the war depend on our preparation to-day, and therefore these preparations must be scrutinised more closely than ever before, with a view to strengthening the efficiency of the armies and of the Governments. The Governments and the Army Commanders are responsible for the failures; a third factor, and in war-time a very momentous one, even in constitutional States, are the dynasties.

19. The Navy

In these reflections only a brief mention has been made of the British Navy; but there are also the French, Italian, and Russian Navies. The four Navies combined could have done a good deal of work if there had been a comprehensive strategic plan.

Perhaps the time for the Navies will come, when Belgium, the Baltic provinces, Austria (Trieste, Pola) and Turkey will be pressed and occupied by the victorious armies of the Allies.

On the whole the decision will be brought about on land.

SECOND PART. *WHAT IS TO BE DONE?*

20. More Soldiers!

If, as I believe, my criticisms have been positive as well as negative (and there is a great difference between the two!), the answer to the question: 'What is to be done?' must be—to avoid or to make good mistakes and, where necessary, to change the methods of procedure, to get the clearest possible insight into the tremendous significance of the present world struggle.

Money—money—and again money, has been described as the principal requisite of war; to-day we must alter this dictum and say: men—men—and again more men! Men, of course, means soldiers.

It is to Russia and Great Britain that we look for the augmentation of the allied armies; the Allies must have larger armies than the enemy at the front, and they must have such reserves of men trained and ready, that a surprise like that in the Balkans shall no longer be possible.

If the French Army is five millions strong, Britain must raise the same number; five millions being the amount of recruits for which she would be liable as a conscript country. Russia must have at least seven millions; that is, compared with Britain and France, a low number, but I take into account the heavy losses of the original Russian Army, especially the heavy losses of officers,* then the financial strength of the country and the productive power of its war industry. As we now can expect that the Allied armies will co-operate, the number of seven millions should be sufficient. These numbers are necessary, for Germany will fight desperately and bring up large quantities. So will Austria, and Turkey will be squeezed by the Germans and will provide further supplies of men. The expense of these huge armies will be fully made good by shortening the war.

In demanding soldiers—more soldiers, we demand by implication more ammunition and the necessary armaments; for soldiers without guns, rifles, high explosives, etc., are no soldiers at all! The Allied troops must undo all the advantages of the Enemy; heavy guns will be needed to destroy his trenches, machine-guns are of the greatest value, etc., etc.

21. Is a Prolonged War advantageous to the Allies?

I know that influential men admonished the English public to be prepared for a long war: a three years', even a twenty years' war has been prognosticated. It is argued that the Allies must neces-

* From a reliable Russian source I was informed that the number of German officers taken prisoners is remarkably low: among the Austrian prisoners one officer out of 60, among the German prisoners one officer out of 560 soldiers! I cannot explain how the German officers could thus escape—at any rate, the German army is adequately supplied with officers (and non-commissioned officers), whereas the Russian and British armies have not enough experienced officers. The French army has enough officers.

sarily win by the prolongation of the war, that Great Britain will be stronger in every respect, and the enemy will be weakened.

I understand quite well, why this argument was brought forward in a country which, owing to her historical development, was not prepared for a war with the Prussian soldiery. I shared this opinion, but only so long as it was necessary to prepare the army; and I doubt whether the enemy has been weakened in the degree supposed. The enemy is also making use of the time available, inventing new kinds of weapons, levying reinforcements, and last, not least, acquiring influence with the Neutrals. The prolongation of the war may easily be taken as hesitation and weakness. A victory only won after long delay is not only far more costly (Sir Edward Carson's argument), but might easily be less efficacious and decisive. But the final victory must be decisive, every kind of drawn game, doubtful for our cause, is a definite victory for the enemy. Having gained unquestioned victories in the initial stages of the war, he must be defeated sufficiently to give in and own his defeat.

The prolongation of the war would affect the financial power of the Allies; it is a question whether Italy, and even France and Russia, could stand the war as long as Britain. The Balkan States are positively afraid of a long war.

France, moreover, having to face the threatening depopulation of the country, will calculate the number of the losses caused by a prolonged every-day war in the trenches.

22. WILL ECONOMICS END THE WAR?

There is a widespread notion that economics, not strategy, will end the war; even officers in leading positions share this opinion. Yet despite the part played by economics, the final decision must inevitably be arrived at on the battlefield.

23. Japan and the War

In France, as I see from several publications, the military help of the Japanese has been seriously considered. National and racial sentiments (the yellow danger) are quite out of place, when once the English and now even the Russians are on friendly terms with Japan. Moreover, the Japanese are our Allies, and have helped already; there is thus no question of principle involved. No doubt the financial aspect would have to be considered. In the first place the transport of the troops to Europe, even to the Turkish theatre of war, would be very expensive. But may not a postponement of the decision prove even more expensive? Perhaps it would be advisable from the political standpoint to bring Japan into a stronger opposition against Germany. In the second place, the Japanese themselves maintain that they cannot accept money payment from the Allies. But the latter would only have to advance to Japan the necessary sum, which would then be repaid out of the future German indemnity. To-day the United States would not interfere with any action of Japan against Germany. However much they may dislike the Japanese, they would certainly prefer Japanese intervention to a German victory.

24. Necessity of a Political as well as a Strategical Plan

King Constantine says in the interview granted to the correspondent of *The Times*: 'We are desirous of knowing the programme which the Allies have drawn up for themselves.' This desire is shared by many people and, it seems, even by the Allies themselves.

In speaking of the plan of the Allies, it is not superfluous to accentuate two things. First, that the strategical plan must be distinguished from the political plan; but it is a matter of course that strategy prepares the political settlement, and the whole war must be subservient to the political aims of the warring States.

On the other hand the political plan influences the strategy, as has been pointed out already.

The second observation refers to Britain. In the English papers and public opinion it is very apparent that the administrative plan of raising an army is mistaken for the strategical plan. In Germany or France this part of the whole task is looked upon as a mere matter of military administration: in England the public pays much greater attention to this work. The difference is very striking. In France, General Joffre, the strategical leader, is put in the foreground and is considered first; while in England, Lord Kitchener's great authority is bound up with military administration, and it is not easy to see who are the supreme strategical leaders of the army. There is no military leader of Joffre's repute. How this affects the army, either men or officers, I have no means of judging, but it is at least suggestive. It is very strange that Lord Kitchener should have had to inspect the East, and to perform the work of a diplomatist. Joffre's visit to London, on the contrary, dealt with matters of strategy. In any case Lord Kitchener's absence points to some vagueness in the supreme war authority.

25. The German Political Programme: Pan-German Central Europe or 'Berlin-Bagdad'

There is a tendency at the present moment to ascribe to the Balkans a high strategical importance, and to imagine that a new epoch of the war is being inaugurated. I do not think so. The theatre of the war has been widened; but from the very beginning it was the Near and the Far East which was aimed at by Germany's outspoken and well-prepared plan, which was and is: *Berlin-Bagdad.*

It is rather curious that this plan should become manifest only now, when Germany is reaching Constantinople. And even to-day the German plan is not fully understood. Yet German politicians, historians and economists have for many years past worked out the plan 'Berlin-Bagdad'. If French, English and

Russian publicists and politicians neglected this plan as an Utopia, they were greatly mistaken. To-day we see, that the German armies have already to a large extent realised the plan.

It is of great importance to know what the German means by 'Berlin-Bagdad'.

Prussia under Bismarck united the greater part of the German nation on the principle of nationality; ever since the eighteenth century the Germans strove to be united, and it was Napoleon who strengthened this craving for unity. So far, the Germans had no other national plan than all the other nations had. Italy claimed her unity at the same time, the Balkan nations were partly freed from Turkey, the nations in Austria tried to weaken German centralism and to get national independence as well.

But the political and national situation of Germany was different from the situation of the Italians, etc. Germany was at first led by the Austrian Habsburgs; but Prussia grew strong, as a result of the Reformation, and by assuming the leadership of the Protestant North, whereas Austria was the leader of the Catholic part of Germany. This rivalry of Prussia and Austria was ended by the defeat of Austria in 1866, and her expulsion from Germany; and this defeat was consummated by the defeat of France in 1870, and the creation of the German Empire.

In this way German national feeling and ideas were embodied in the Pan-German Programme. This programme claimed in the first place the incorporation of Austria into the new empire; but Bismarck opposed the Pan-Germans on the ground that Germany could not stand the accretion of Catholics (to-day there are 42 millions of Protestants as against 25 millions Catholics: the incorporation of Austria would add another 25 millions Catholics, and thus give Germany a Catholic majority). Bismarck's plan, therefore, was to leave Austria-Hungary independent, but to use her as an ally. That is the real meaning of the Triple Alliance. Lagarde, the father of modern Pan-Germanism, interpreted Bismarck's plan in the sense that Austria must be Germany's colony and 'Hinterland', and that Trieste must be preserved for Germany.

Italy, as a member of the Triple Alliance, had to check her Irredenta, just in the same way that the Pan-German Irredenta was checked by the intimate Alliance of Germany with Austria.

Bismarck succeeded in winning Hungary (Andrássy) for his plan, and in inducing even official Austria to accept his scheme, though there was always a section of the Austrian-Germans (the so-called 'Alt-Oesterreicher') who did not accept Pan-Germanism, and the Dynasty had also shown considerable reluctance. By degrees the leaders of Pan-Germanism came to accept Bismarck's and Lagarde's scheme. It is a mistake to suppose that Bismarck and Pan-Germanism exclude each other: Prince Bülow, in his treatise on Politics, shows that Bismarck, had he lived, would have followed the Pan-German Programme. In fact, the leaders of Pan-Germanism proclaim now and during the war that they fully accept Bismarck's practical scheme.

The Pan-German Programme claimed in the name of nationality not only Austria but also Hungary, with over two millions of Germans (the Saxons in Transylvania, and the Swabians of the Banat), the Russian Baltic provinces, German Switzerland—even Holland, proclaiming Dutch as a German dialect. Using the word 'Germanism' in its wider sense, the Germans claim the leadership of not only the German-Teutons but of the whole Germanic race, including the Scandinavians and the English. Poland was demanded on the ground that there were many German colonies. By degrees the Pan-German plan was transformed into the project of Central Europe led by Germany. Germany accepted Turkey as a new ally, aining not only at the Balkans but at Asia-Minor as well; 'Berlin-Bagdad' became the watchword of this enlarged Pan-German scheme.

The German antagonism against Russia and France, the growing antagonism against Great Britain completed the Pan-German scheme. So Holland, Switzerland were to be annexed to the Customs Union of Central Europe, the so-called German Baltic Provinces—the population of which, as a matter of fact, is Lettish, only the aristocracy and the townspeople being German—were to be 'liberated'. Furthermore the growing Ruthenian (Ukrainian) movement was to be used against Russia, a Ruthenian State was to be formed in the East as a buffer against Russia, needless to say as yet another member of the Germanised Zollverein. The Balkan States with their German princes and princesses (excepting Serbia and Montenegro) were regarded merely as natural satellites of Germany.

Besides these nationalistic and economic incitements to world power, Germany was stimulated by England's example. The Pan-German literature clearly shows it, and the Germans admit it openly enough; it is England who inspired the building of a great Navy, it was England's industry and commerce which incited to competition on the world's market; it is the British Empire which roused Germany's envy and political emulation. Finally the very idea of the German Empire, as the sequel and continuation of the Roman Empire, and the renovation of this Empire was the political programme of World Power and the declaration of 'the will to power'.

Under the given circumstances Britain and Russia, the two World Powers, were the natural opponents of these German aspirations; but both Russia and Britain very often helped Germany in achieving her plan either involuntarily or even voluntarily—no doubt assuming that Germany only aimed at the position of an equal among equals. But soon it became manifest that Germany aspires to lead the world; it was to prevent Russia's full development and reorganisation which began after the Russo-Japanese War, that Germany waged this war, thinking that England would not join the Entente.

This grand scheme of Berlin-Bagdad was drawn up and elaborated by the Pan-German politicians; there are numerous authors of untiring energy, who popularised these political aspirations realised finally in the present war, for Germany controls practically at this moment the area of the Pan-German 'Central Europe'.

In the nineties, the Pan-German Programme was worked out

in detail, the German Central Europe and the *Weltreich* was fully shaped. Soon the watchword 'Berlin-Bagdad' was circulated in books and the press. Not only Bronsart von Schellendorf, the Prussian War Minister, but the Kaiser himself is an ardent adherent of Pan-Germanism and a pupil of Lagarde. Bronsart gave a detailed programme of Central Europe under Germany's leading. And the scheme, Berlin-Bagdad, first began to be shaped by men like List and Moltke, and can be traced back to Frederick the Great and his Turkish policy.

Now that Germany has succeeded in occupying the territory forming the essential part of the Pan-German programme of Central Europe or 'Berlin-Bagdad'—not only Pan-Germanism, but the whole development of Prussia-Germany must be reviewed and revised in accordance with the present situation on the battle-fields.

26. Austria and the Magyars as the tools and puppets of Pan-Germanism

Austria's significance for Germany must be obvious to all to-day. 'Berlin-Bagdad' means above all the abdication of Austria-Hungary as a really independent State.

Germany went into the war as a 'loyal' ally of Austria-Hungary; but to-day Germany is not an ally, she is the military leader, the political and economic sovereign of 'independent' Austria-Hungary. Germany has the 51 millions of the population of Austria-Hungary at her disposal. Austria-Hungary opens up the road from Berlin to Constantinople; it is the 'Alliance' with Austria-Hungary which has enabled Germany to invade the Balkans.

The direct Alliance with Turkey and Bulgaria and the invasion of the Balkans is the consequence of the full mastery over Austria-Hungary. It is a riddle to me how the politicians in England, France, and Russia could fail to grasp the true meaning of the Triple Alliance, and above all of the peaceful penetration of

Austria-Hungary by Germany; they of course paid no attention to the struggle of the Austrian Slavs against the oppressive influence of Germany, nor did they notice the national efforts of Bohemia and the Southern Slavs. So short-sighted were they that they even patronised the principal instrument of Germany, the Magyars, who had skilfully acquired control of Austria's diplomatic service. Latterly all the more important Austro-Hungarian Embassies have been held by Magyars, the outspoken adherents and tools of Germany, and the Magyar aristocrats influenced and created political opinion not only of the diplomatists, but also actually of the Governments of the Entente Powers.

In France, it is true, some sympathies were tendered to the Bohemians, and even some practical advances were tried. In Russia the official world was very little touched by the theories and practices of the unofficial Slavophils. Only the Balkan Slavs, the Orthodox Bulgars and Serbs, were officially acknowledged, as also the Greeks.

To-day at least it must be evident that the present situation in the Balkans is the logical outcome of Pan-Germanism; the way to Bagdad was secured and fortified on the battlefields in Russia and France—Belgium. There the dice for Bagdad, for Asia and Africa were cast, and will be cast again.

27. The War in the Balkans: the three Allied Powers—Britain, France, and Russia—must rely on themselves

It would be a mistake to say, that the war in the Balkans is secondary—no, it is the continuation of the war in the North. But the decision of the war, and that means, the decision as to the leadership in Europe and Asia, will be fought out in Russia and France. It is a matter of course that the Balkans must be defended by the Allies too. They must send there enough troops to prevent the Germans from occupying Constantinople, encouraging Persia and threatening Egypt and India.

Nevertheless, and in spite of the need for defending Constantinople and the Balkans (Serbia)—one very serious lesson follows from the general situation: the three great Allies must depend on themselves, and on themselves only.

I have said that the question, whether the diplomatists have brought the bad situation in the Balkans upon the Allies, is now of no great consequence. But I go still further. The very fact that they are blaming the diplomatists, proves that they do not grasp the situation, and that they are accusing the Allies of a great weakness. The perpetual negotiations with Greece and Roumania, and with Bulgaria, the whole campaign in the Press, is a lamentable proof that this weakness is not merely diplomatic.

The development of the war and the attitude of the neutrals should have been better understood. One victory in France or Russia, even a moderate victory, will do more than any number of diplomatic démarches. German diplomacy has triumphed in the Balkans, because the German arms have been victorious. Turkey's adherence to Germany was a very strong example and suggestion for all the Eastern States and Nations. The hesitation and Germanophil tendencies of the other Balkan and Asiatic States are the natural result of Turkey's example. Bulgaria's decision after a long period of hesitation, and the hesitation of Greece—is it possible not to see into the situation?

The Allies were guilty of a great strategic fault in allowing themselves to be surprised by Germany's march to aid her Turkish ally; they ought to have had such reserves of men as to render any surprise impossible. It is to be hoped they will not be surprised once more in Mesopotamia, Armenia and Egypt.

The war is a war of the Great Powers of Europe; the small States are neutral, and will join one side or the other, according to the situation on the battlefield.

Britain, France and Russia must be able to defeat Germany, Austria and Turkey—therefore Britain and Russia must raise the necessary armies, if France has already brought up her full quota of men.

28. The Political Programme of the Allies: Non-German, Anti-German, European Central Europe: Liberty of all nations, also of small nations

The political plan of Germany must be counterbalanced by a political plan of the Allies. But until now, the Allies had no such plan, each had a special plan of his own. France aims at the recovery of Alsace-Lorraine. England defended her naval supremacy, and Russia was eager to incorporate East Galicia. *That* was the real plan. The liberation of Belgium and of the small nations is a very noble, and a very practical programme; but hitherto it has merely been proclaimed in the abstract. The policy of the Allies is not directed by that programme.

The Allies must meet the German plan of Central Europe controlled by Germany, by the plan of Central Europe freed from German control. In my lecture on the Small Nations* I have attempted to show that Central Europe contains a peculiar zone of smaller, unfree or half free nations, and that the political organisation of this zone is the real task of the present war.

The Germans have grasped the vital importance of this ethnographical zone of Central Europe: their plan of Central Europe controlled by Germany has been conceived from the German standpoint. The tactics may change according to the situation: *divide et impera* was the rule up to now; for some time past they have been trying to persuade the nations of Central Europe that Germany is their best friend, that the Germans aspire to the ruling control, not only in her own interest but also in the interests of these nations themselves.

At any rate it is obvious that the German plan of Central Europe is a far-reaching and grandiose plan; the Allies must have an equally far-reaching plan for the treatment of Central Europe.

* See *The Problem of Small Nations in the European Crisis.* (Council for Study of International Relations.)

And the German plan is not only grandiose and far-reaching, but it is at the same time practical: the Allies must have an equally practical programme.

29. Independent Poland—Independent Bohemia—Independent Greater Serbia

This plan of the Allies can only consist in an energetic endeavour to liberate the Non-German nations of Central Europe.

Central Europe comprises the East of Germany, Austria-Hungary, the Balkans and the Western part of Russia (Poland). The restoration and liberation of Poland, of Bohemia comprising the Slovak country of North Hungary, and the organisation of Greater Serbia is the first and essential task of the Allies; all other questions will be solved easily if the Allies perform this task.

Free Poland with independent Bohemia is the direct check against Prussia.

Very often it is proclaimed that the Allies are going to crush Prussian Militarism. How is that to be achieved? If this plan has a practical meaning, it can only consist of the plan to weaken Prussia directly and permanently by liberating the Poles and Czechs, and creating buffer States against Prussian aggression. Free Poland reaching to the Baltic would make East Prussia an enclave, as it was in the past, and Germany would be proportionately weakened.

The significance of Independent Bohemia may be seen from the history and the geographical position of the country. The Bohemians were strong enough to resist the German *Drang nach Osten*; it was the union with Bohemia which made Austria so strong and powerful. Bismarck observed very rightly, that the possession of Bohemia guarantees the dominion over Europe. The liberation of Bohemia is, for the Allies, as important as the liberation of Poland and the Southern Slavs. In fact these three tasks must form the main object of a sound anti-German policy on the part of the Allies.

Of course Austria-Hungary must be dismembered. It can and must be manifest now that any scheme for the preservation of Austria-Hungary is a direct form of 'travail pour le roi de Prusse', for Austria-Hungary has proved herself, and that not only during the war but before it, to be a mere instrument in the hands of Germany. It is the Pan-German plan to preserve Austria-Hungary.

The liberation and union of the Southern Slavs under the political guidance of Serbia would mean a further stage in the dismemberment of Austria-Hungary, and in the organic remodelling of the Balkans on a racial basis. And surely Serbia has proved her loyalty as an Ally!

Italy's just national aspirations also demand the dismemberment of Austria-Hungary. Italy would be then the neighbour of Greater Serbia, and would complete the anti-German barrier formed by Poland, Bohemia and Greater Serbia.

Further, the organisation of a *Magyar* as opposed to a *Hungarian* State and the liberation of the Hungarian and Austrian Roumanians are necessary political corollaries.

There still remains the question of Constantinople and of European and Asiatic Turkey. Can the Allies come to an understanding on this vexed question?

30. Germany's weak spot is in the East

Germany's weak spot is in the East, not in the West. By liberating and organising the smaller nations of Central Europe against German aggression Germany will be weakened in the West also, and that is the only way.

Germany's historical *Drang nach Osten* must be checked and stopped—that is the task of Russia and her Western Allies. Germany when driven out of the East, will not be strong in the West. It was Bismarck who proclaimed that the Polish East has a greater significance for Germany than Alsace-Lorraine. France, the principal west Continental country, claims a comparatively small rectification of her frontier.

Holland, Denmark, and Belgium are populous countries, countries economically and culturally equal to Germany, and even in certain directions on a higher level; Germany, even if she could subdue these nations, would not find the colonies and 'Hinterland' that she longs for, nor would she find a working class which was helpless and at her mercy, as in the East. Moreover, these Western countries, in the event of German aggression, would always find France and Britain on their side, just as now Britain has protected Belgium—of course protecting herself at the same time. There can be no doubt that Germany in already controlling Luxemburg, eagerly looks to Antwerp and to the Channel coast, and at the same time looks with disfavour upon Denmark. But it is safe to assume that Germany's pressure on the West will be all the stronger and keener, if she has a huge economic Hinterland easily accessible on her eastern frontier.

Hence to contend that by liberating Central Europe the Allies would cut off Germany from the East, and thus force her to press the harder against the West, is an argument much more apparent than real. On the contrary, Germany cut off from the East, and no longer having Austria-Hungary and the Balkans at her disposal, would be forced to rely upon her own forces, and would cease to be a danger to the West. Germany would be forced to revert to the agricultural pursuits which she has abandoned; her surplus population would be forced to emigrate, as in the past. The Eastern nations, Poland, Russia, etc., are under no obligation to render it possible for the German butcher, grocer, or professor to rear the largest possible family for the 'inferior' nations of Eastern Europe to supply with food.

31. France and Russia—Britain and Russia

Viewed from this standpoint, the Franco-Russian Alliance has a greater significance than the mere negative and anti-German role ascribed to it by German politicians and historians. That it is anti-German is natural enough; for French and Russian politicians perceived the real situation of Germany and the meaning of her *Drang nach Osten*, and combined a programme to protect and liberate the Slav nations of Central Europe.

Britain's accession to the Franco-Russian alliance proves the very same political idea. The fact that the long antagonism of Britain and Russia was bridged over, is an even clearer proof that the political evolution of Central Europe has been forcing upon the two former rivals a perception of the identity of their national and political interests. As so often happens in politics, the first overture was made in a secondary and local field (Persia, etc.), but the march of events widened the plan and brought out its real underlying idea. An idea, at first abstract and unclear, has to be put into concrete forms and clearly worked out. But in this case events so precipitated themselves, and the war took Russia and England so completely by surprise, that there has been practically no time to think out a political programme.

The German politicians perceive the real inner meaning of the Anglo-Russian agreement. More than once during the war they remembered Bismarck's attitude towards Russia. It is not difficult to detect in many utterances of prominent German publicists and politicians (among others of Hindenburg himself) a hidden appeal to Russia. Russia and Germany, even a victorious Germany and a defeated Russia, would by their mere union be able to partition Europe and Asia.

But the Russians know that they would be a mere tool of Pan-German aspirations; and both Russian and British statesmen will agree that the liberation of Poland and Bohemia and the organisation of a Greater Serbia suits not only British and French, but also Russian political plans every bit as well. Germany separated from Russia will be weakened.

32. Austria and Germany once more

Often an objection is made that the dismemberment of Austria-Hungary would strengthen Germany: questions are put as to what would become of the Germans in Austria, and what Francis Joseph would do? Obviously it is Francis Joseph's own business to take care of himself and to decide, whether he will continue to be the tool of Germany or not. Some politicians were even harassed by the question, what title the Austrian Emperor would have!

I look at all these questions of New Europe from a liberal and democratic standpoint. The Austrian Emperor, if he chooses, can continue to be Emperor of Austria, as the Byzantine Emperors kept their Imperial title even after their dominion was more reduced than Austria would be.

And supposing that German Austria were to become in one or other way a member of the German Empire. In that case Germany would have at her disposal only ten extra millions, whereas Austria, if only reduced but not dismembered, would strengthen Germany twice or three times as much. The very idea, that after the war Austria will be inclined to go against Germany, is simply naïve. Only one thing can be expected: Catholic Austria, if included in Germany, would naturally weaken Protestant Prussia.

The same remark holds good for Hungary. The Magyars will be forced to renounce their anti-Slav policy, if once the Slavs are free and under the protection of the Allies. But, of course, the plan of the Allies pre-supposes their victory and the defeat of the enemy, who until now has been victorious.

33. How Germany's defeat and retreat would take place

Very often this victory is belittled. Our papers, publicists and politicians try to keep up their spirit by explaining away the enemy's achievements. This old-fashioned method strikes me as less effective than its adherents suppose. It is always dangerous to underrate the enemy. The truth is, that the Germans have won a great victory, and that it will be a heavy task to defeat them. How, then, is that defeat to be accomplished?

The first phase of the German defeat would be accomplished, when they will have to retire from the occupied territories; after that the second phase would follow, the invasion of the Allies into Germany, Austria, Turkey and Bulgaria.

If the first task is difficult the second will be even more so. Especially the Germans will fight very desperately to prevent the occupation of their territory. In the East and in the West the frontier is already fortified by trenches, and every possible means of defence is provided. The Germans will fight fiercely to the very last, and will not be demoralised by having to retire to their own soil. The Austrian troops will be weaker in that respect, and doubtless the same holds good with the Bulgarians and Turks. Yet it must not be forgotten that the Austrians have also fortified and prepared some parts of their territory; the passes into Hungary from Galicia are fortified, Cracow and Moravia, Vienna and Budapest are fortified also.

Germany, if pressed by the Allies, would withdraw her forces from Austria and the Balkans, would abandon her Allies and defend her territory with all available forces. The fighting line would be considerably shortened; the resistance would be stronger. It will be very difficult in the West to cross the Rhine; in the East is the ominous East Prussian lake country, while both the Silesian coal mines and the collieries and the industrial centres of Rhenish Prussia will be defended very fiercely. The Germans expect that France would be satisfied with the occupation of Alsace-Lorraine, and that she would not sacrifice her troops to invade the Trans-Rhenish territories. The occupation of Berlin would be, of course, a hard piece of strategical work. Personally, I had expected the Allies to penetrate from the Balkans towards Budapest and Vienna; I expected that the Serbians, backed by the Allies, would be able to occupy Zagreb (Agram). Even now the Allies could make use of the Balkans by marching against Hungary-Austria, the Russians proceeding from the East; in that case the

Roumanians would join—but for this we need soldiers, soldiers, soldiers!

The Russians were expected to occupy the North of Hungary, Moravia and Bohemia; that will be their task again, for the occupation of these countries is of great political significance. The occupation of Vienna or Berlin is more of a demonstrative character, whereas the occupation of Alsace-Lorraine, Poznan (Posen) and Prussian Silesia, Galicia, Moravia, Bohemia and of Croatia in the South has a great significance as a first step towards the organisation of Central Europe on anti-German lines.

The occupation of the Slav countries of Germany and Austria-Hungary is the end of Pan-German imperialism; Austria-Hungary is the weakest point of Germany, every weakening of Austria is a blow to Germanism.

Often the expectation is expressed that Germany will rapidly collapse after the first defeat. I can only re-affirm my scepticism in that respect. But it is probable that Austria would not stand a serious blow very well.

34. The Neutrals and Germany's defeat

A decisive victory of the Allies, especially of the Russians, would soon induce Roumania to join the Allies, and perhaps Greece as well. It will depend on the intensity of the Allies' victory whether Denmark would not march against Germany to recover the lost Danish territory; Holland's help could be expected to assist in the recovery of Belgium. The diplomatists will have an opportunity of atoning for their shortcomings in the past.

35. The economic significance of Free Central Europe: Boycott of Germany

The strategic and political defeat of Pan-German imperialism and the liberation of Central Europe must be intensified by an economic defence.

Britain, Austria-Hungary, Russia, France, and the United States; then Belgium and Holland, Australia and Denmark had the largest trade with Germany. The Allies could, therefore, by special treaties prepare the economic boycott of Germany.

The dismemberment of Austria-Hungary, and the creation of the new States of Poland, Bohemia and Greater Serbia will affect the international market; the industry of Poland and Bohemia would be open to Russia and the Balkans; Danzig as a Polish port would be of great significance for Russia, Denmark, Sweden and for Britain. Not merely Salonica and Constantinople, but also Trieste, Fiume and Spalato on the Adriatic would increase in importance as commercial centres.

The economic and financial exhaustion of belligerents and neutrals alike will give to the United States an opportunity of interfering in Europe; the financial policy of the United States will be able to promote new political schemes. Once more the diplomatists will have a new field of activity.

But—the first demand is, and must be, to form a plan as clear as possible for the political and economic re-shaping of Europe in the future. Bismarck condemned every war in which the possible fruits of victory have not been considered before the war is in progress. Bismarck initiated three wars (against Denmark, Austria and France), and all these wars were a success not least of all because they were the means to a well-shaped and grand political plan. The Allies also must have a well-shaped and grand political plan. They have, in fact, proclaimed the liberation of Europe and of the smaller nations from Pan-Germanism and Prussian militarism, and that is a grand and noble plan; but it still has to be clearly worked out in detail.

On the battlefields, of course, strength and force decide, strength and force as they have been accumulated in years, centuries, ages; one of the forces acting and deciding is our conception of history, the capability and aptitude to understand the direction which historic development has taken, and the strong will to shape the future of our own nation and of Europe as a whole. I never could agree with those critics of Pan-Germanism, who sneered at the ink-wasting German generals like Frobenius, Bernhardi, Eichhorn, Keim, Bronsart, right back to the days of Moltke. These generals prepared this war, and their writings are as essential a part of German preparedness as their stocks of ammunition. Our leaders in the war must have a clear idea as to the direction in which they wish their own nation and Europe as a whole to develop. The war is not only a display of blind forces, but also of intelligence, insight and knowledge. Knowledge is Power.

The programme of the Allies cannot be a mere plan to crush Germany; for a nation of 65 millions (with German Austria 75 millions) cannot be crushed. It must be a plan of defence, a plan for promoting the moral and political progress of Europe and of Humanity. It is a plan to force Germany to be human, to accept and to comprehend the humanitarian programme of the best German thinkers. Germany, when she has abandoned the ferocious philosophy of the superman and the policy of the 'blonde beast' aspiring to the bloodstained dominion of mankind, will easily find her place as an equal among equals.

INDEX

Accurti, 17
Adler, Friedrich, 101
Adriatic Question, 131
Aehrenthal, Count, 17, 35
Alsace-Lorraine, 193, 199
Andrássy, Count, 188
Arbeiter-Zeitung, 58
Army, Allied, 159
  Austro-Hungarian, 158
  British, 188
  French, 175
  Russian, 177
Asquith, Mr, 21, 73, 135
Atter, Robert, 35
Austria, artificial character of, 122
Austria-Hungary, dismemberment of, 194, 201

Baerlein, Mr H., 24
Bahr, Hermann, 80
Baird, Major, 85
Baker, James, 60
Bakunin, 11
Balkans, war in, 67, 191
Barclay, Sir George, 50
Belgium, 49, 52, 192, 196
Benckendorff, Count, 34
Beneš, Dr E., 2, 13, 21, 22, 23, 28, 56, 71, 73, 82
  Madame E., 22
  Vojta, 96
Berchtold, Count, 19
Berlin-Bagdad, 78, 88, 121, 151, 186, 190
Bethmann Hollweg, 77, 89
Bismarck, 4, 120, 133, 187, 195, 201
Bohemia and Austria, 46, 127
Bohemia and Russia, 43
Bolsheviks, Masaryk and, 105
Bolshevisation, 12
Bošković, M., 67
Boy-Ed, 97
Briand, Aristide, 83, 176
Britain, role of, 48
Bryce, Lord, 72
Buchanan, Sir G., 87
Bülow, Prince, 188
Burke, Edmund, 16
Burrows, R. M., 39, 68–9, 70, 85, 154
Business as Usual, 172

Caesaropapism, 11, 27
Çanaan, Jonescu, 80
Čapek, Karel, 11, 13, 15, 32
Caporetto, 24
Çarson, Sir Edward, 184
Čas, 1
Cecil, Lord, 21, 72, 92
Censorship, 155
Charles, Archduke, 16
  Emperor of Austria, 7
Charles IV, Emperor, 7
Chelčický, Peter, 7, 30, 149
Chéradame, André, 91
Chirol, Sir V., 36
Choc, M., 47
Chotek, Countess, 19
Christian Socialists, 9
Clerk, Mr George, 39, 50, 57, 61, 74
Comenius, 32
Conrad von Hötzendorf, 59
Constance, Council of, 5
Constantine, King of Greece, 185
Constantinople, 132
Constitution, Bohemian, 133
Corfu, declaration of, 103
Corridor, Czech-Jugoslav, 129
Crane, Mr Charles, 35
Creighton, Bishop, 5
Crewe, Lord, 173
Croatia, Masaryk and, 15
Ctesiphon battle, 172
Cyril, St, 5
Czech Renaissance, 6

Dalmatia and Italy, 59, 65, 66, 130
Dardanelles, 173
Darwin, 73
Delbrück, Hans, 77
Delcassé, Théophile, 21, 39, 62
Democracy, 27, 177
Denis, Ernest, 51, 71, 125
Dickens, 32
Dobrovsky, 7
Dostoyevsky, 13
Drang nach Osten, 194, 197
Dualism, 8, 123
Dumba, Constantin, 99
Dürich, 65
Dvořák, 9

Economic meaning of Free Central Europe, 200
Economics and War, 184
'Eleventh Hour, At the', 49, 76
English Review, 27
Eucharistic Congress, 13
'European Review', 35

Federalism, 20
Feuerbach, 11
Fiedler, Dr, 35, 80
Fisher, H. A. L., 148
Fitzwilliams, Major, 104
Forgács, Count, 17
Fox, Charles James, 16
Francis Ferdinand, Archduke, 19
Francis Joseph, 8, 43, 59, 198
Francis Salvator, Archduke, 81
Frankfurt, 7
Frederick, Archduke, 65
Friedjung trial, 17, 57
Frontier Plans, 44, 52

Galicia, East, 193
Galliéni, Gen., 155
Gallipoli, 173
Gebauer, 14
German colonising policy, 3
German war-plan, 162
Germany and Russia, 45
Goebbels, Dr, 15
Goethe, 19
Goričar, Dr, 78, 97
Grey, Sir Edward, 39, 61, 87
Grouard, Colonel, 175
Grünberg MS, 14

Hammerling, 98
Havlíček, Karel, 7
Hayn, Dr, 42
Hegel, 11, 13
Hej Slovaní, 34, 40
Henry, Sir Edward, 74
Herrenvolk, 21, 73, 145
Herron, Prof., 113
Hervé, Gustave, 177
Hilsner, Leopold, 15
Hindenburg, 90, 178, 197
Hindus, Mr Maurice, 3
Hinković, Dr, 113
Hitler, 7, 15, 19
Hoare, Sir Samuel, 87
Hodža, Dr Milan, 29
Hohenlohe, Prince, 81, 91
Hume, David, 12
Hurban Vajanský, 5, 35
Hus, John, 7, 30, 64, 71, 133, 148

Japan, 185
Jesuits, 17
Jesus, not Caesar, 12, 13, 27
Jews in Prague, 41
Jungman, 7

Kant, 11
Kiel Canal, 77
King's College, 39
Kitchener, 21, 55, 75
Klofáč, V., 42, 47
Kollár, Jan, 7, 28, 148
Königinhof MS, 14
Kopecky, F., 60
Kosovo, 150
Košutić, Dr, 16
Kramář, Dr, 22, 25, 42, 47, 54, 65
Krofta, Dr, 30
Kut, 85

Lagarde, 121, 146, 187
Lány, 32
Leeper, Mr R. A., 103

Legions, Czechoslovak, 2, 24, 35, 101, 106, 110, 111
Liberals, German, 9
Lloyd George, Mr, Masaryk on, 91
London, Treaty of, 59, 62
Long war, advantages of, 183
'Los von Rom', 9
Losky, 25
Lowell, Russell, 26
Lusitania, the, 100
Luther, 5
Lützow, Count Francis, 57

Machar, 56
Mackensen, 81
Maffia, Czech, 28
Magyars, 8, 122, 148, 188, 195, 198
Manchester Guardian, 62
Marchant, F. P., 60
Marne battle, 176
Marxism, Masaryk on, 13
Masaryk, Alice, 22, 29, 79
  Jan, 58
  Olga, 60, 147
Maticé Česká, 9
Mattuš, Dr, 20
Mesopotamia, 172
Meštrović, Ivan, 55
Methodius, St, 5
Military Attachés, 181
Milyukov, Prof., 34, 101, 103
Mişu, N., 10
Mobilisation figures, 157
'Modus Vivendi', 12
Moravia, Great, 2
Münsterberg, Prof., 90
Myasoyedov, Col., 67, 163, 179

Napier, Col., 50
Naše Doba, 1, 18
Nation Tchèque, 125
Nationality, Principle of, 117
Naumann, Friedrich, 86
Navy, British, 182
New Europe, 87, 89, 101, 107
New Statesman, 76, 86
Novi List, 67
Nowak, K. F., 63

Orthodoxy, 4
Osuský, Dr S., 22, 113

Pacelli, Cardinal, 13
Paderewski, Ignaz, 113
Paget, Lady Muriel, 104
Palacký, F., 7, 8, 124, 127, 148
Pan-Germanism, 85, 88, 143, 146, 161, 186
Panslavism, 4
Papen, Herr von, 97
Paragraph Fourteen, 9
Pares, Sir Bernard, 87
Pašić, Nicholas, 19
'Pater Patriae', 2, 32
Petrograd, 179
Philadelphia, 2, 113
Pius XII, 12
Podiebrad, George of, 7
Points, Fourteen, 14, 25
Poland and Russia, 25, 45, 194
Poles in Germany, 77
Population figures, 156

Rašín, A., 22, 29, 71, 79
Realists, Czech, 1, 18
Realpolitik, 73
Recognition, 105, 108
Rieger, F. X., 14, 80, 147
Rodd, Sir Rennell, 65
Rome Congress, 24
Rotterdam, 20, 36–8, 63
Roumanian mobilisation plan, 128
Round Table, 76
Russell, Bertrand, 89
Russia, climate of, 166
Russia and Germany, 197
Russky, General, 166

Safářik, R. J., 7
Salonica, 174
Sazonov, Serge, 21, 34, 39, 59
Scheiner, Dr, 22, 65
Schellendorf, Bronsart von, 190
School of Slavonic Studies, 21, 68, 135, 152
Schulverein, Deutscher, 9
Scotland Yard, 74, 100
Sea Power, 119

Serbian Relief Fund, 36, 68
'Serbo-Croatia', 129
Shakhmatov, 102
Slavic barrier, 130
Slovak and Czech, 61
Small Nations, Masaryk on, 21, 72, 93, 118, 126, 135–52, 193
Smith, Mr Nowell, 26
Sokols, 9, 47, 66, 103
Sonnino, Baron, 65
Spalajković, M., 66, 103
Spirit of Russia, 11
Spitzmüller, Dr, 81
Šrobár, Dr V., 29
Stalin, M., 4, 102
Steed, Mr Wickham, 27, 33, 34, 36, 61, 63, 65, 74, 85, 107, 114
Sturdza, Conrad, 50
Stürgkh, Count, 101
Sully, Eugene, 60
Superstate and Superman, 150
Supilo, Frano, 17, 36, 52, 55, 59, 67
Švehla, A., 29, 47
Switzerland, a monarchical, 20
Sykora, J., 60

Tannenberg, 67
Tarabocchia, 17
Tersztyanszky, Gen., 81
Theatre, Czech National, 9
Thompson, Sir Basil, 100
Thun, Prince, 40
Times, The, 33, 36, 48, 62, 64, 180, 185
Tobolka, 80
Tolstoy, 7, 149
Townshend, Gen., 173
Treitschke, H. v., 133, 146
Trentino, 59
Trevelyan, G. M., 36
Trieste, 121, 131, 187
Trotsky, 111
Trumbić, Ante, 55, 67
Tyrš, Miroslav, 9

Ukrainians, 109, 179, 189
'Unitas Fratrum', 5
University of Prague, 4, 10
Urban, Dr, 80

Valona, 53, 66
Vasić, 19
Venizelos, E., 92
Villa Giusti, 114
Vinogradoff, Prof., 31, 39
Viškovsky, 89
Vojnović, Lujo, 55
Voska, Emanuel, 34, 87, 96

Wahrmund, Prof., 19, 35
Weekly, The, 84
Wenceslas, St, 5, 13
White Mountain, 6, 123
Whyte, Sir F., 29
William II, Emperor, 90
Williams, Harold, 87
Wilson, President, 2, 25, 91, 94–5, 108, 113

Young Czechs, 8, 42

Zagreb Trial, 15, 16, 35, 199
Zborov, 24
Živković, Gen., 102
Žižka, 7, 149
Zone of Small Nations, 140